business data processing

Edited by Ronald B Yearsley

Computers and the Unions

Clive Jenkins and Barrie Sherman

Longman
London and New York

Longman Group Limited London

Associated companies, branches and representatives throughout the world

Published in the United States of America by Longman Inc., New York

First published 1977

Library of Congress Cataloging in Publication Data

Jenkins, Clive.
Computers and the unions.

(Business data processing)
1. Electronic data processing and industrial relations. 2. Electronic data processing – Economic aspects – Great Britain. 3. Trade-unions – Great Britain – Data processing. I. Sherman, Barrie, joint author. II. Title.
HD6971.J46 1977 331.88'12'1381950941 76–12098
ISBN 0 582 45017 9

Set in IBM Journal 10 on 11pt
and printed in Great Britain by
Richard Clay (The Chaucer Press) Ltd,
Bungay, Suffolk

Contents

1 Introducing computers and unions 1
2 The computers about us 10
3 Computers, people and jobs 20
4 The public face 31
5 Changing patterns 38
6 Collective bargaining 46
7 Unions meet the computer 56
8 Bargaining digitally 69
9 More or less jobs 77
10 Unions use computers too 84
11 Checks and balances 92
12 Shaping society 103
13 Who benefits: Them or us? 112
14 Force for good or force for evil? 121

Index 131

Chapter 1

Introducing computers and unions

Computers are man-made tools and as such are in the direct line of descent from the earliest flint axeheads. The main difference to those who used or were affected by them, lies in the fact that Stone-Age man could understand the axe or knife, and later medieval man could understand the harrow and gunpowder but today all too few people understand the computer. As technology advances so specialisation increases; in medicine there are now at least twenty specialities each of which appropriate a jargon and knowledge which precludes understanding even to other doctors and technicians. Computers have not only developed from such a specialisation but, like medicine, have built up a defensive wall of language calculated to mystify all but the initiated.

The job of a tool is to aid man in performing tasks, either by enabling them to be done more quickly, or with more ease, or to open new fields of operation which would otherwise remain closed. The computer does all of these. There are few facets of life in an industrialised country, such as Britain, which are unaffected by the computer, although such involvement often goes unnoticed by the population in general. Notice is taken however, when mistakes are made; and mistakes there are. Horror stories abound; electricity bills for £10,000 for an old-age pensioner in the summer quarter; four tax demands for different amounts presented on the same day; continuing bills for cancelled magazines, indeed the uncancellability of some journals; salaries diminishing slowly to zero; predictions of the economy so wrong that tea-leaves would appear to be a better method of forecasting. It is at these times that people realise that computers help in paying wages, assist mailing, arrange seat bookings, etc.; at all other times only the final service is recognised; the means of providing that service are neither known nor cared about.

These errors must often arise because computers are merely tools used by man, and even if the machine is perfect man is fallible. Information has to be fed in to be stored; the correct questions have to be asked to get the right answers; the right assumptions made to get realistic predictions. In the trade the description is 'garbage in – garbage out': what we must avoid is becoming a nation of refuse collectors.

Lack of knowledge is often accompanied by fear – the unknown has always been a potent force. Computers are the subject of much suspicion and mistrust as well as fear. This is partly due to the inevitable concern any new wide-ranging concept engenders (for example, the insistence on a man with a red flag preceding the early motor-cars was inspired by the fear of their unbridled speed and power) but also partly due to those who work with computers themselves. Instead of explaining the new, advertising its advantages and stressing its benefits, a smokescreen of terminology is thrown up of 'hard-ware', 'soft-ware', 'data-bases' and 'interfaces' for all the world like a cross between a costumiers and a cosmetics firm. This is not what computers are about. Computers are about helping man to live a better life, for this is what tools are about. The problem is that computers, like nuclear energy, are double-edged; on one side they are of potentially great benefit; on the other side capable of harming mankind itself, if not physically then morally and spiritually.

Computers affect our everyday lives. The working lives of some people are directly affected, others indirectly, but for most if not all there are direct and indirect influences in day-to-day matters. Therefore computers deserve our attention; they are too important and too all-pervasive to be ignored. The clock cannot be turned back. As much as some people would like to revert to the simpler pre-automative age and yearn for the simple productive methods and distributive systems of the 'good old days' it will take a cataclysmic event for these to return. Like it or not computers are here to stay.

Computers are machines which store information, can retrieve information if asked to do so, and can manipulate information if given the correct and precise instructions. The information which goes into the computer (the input) is generally no different from that stored in files or on cards in non-computerised concerns. The retrieval and manipulation of the information, both arranged by programming the computer can be done either by manual or technical means. The advantage of this lies in the speed with which given tasks can be performed and often the reduction in manpower required to do these tasks. A computer is not necessarily more accurate in its final output – the result depends on operators, programmers and analysts defining the right questions and then performing all their tasks accurately. The machine itself may function well but so may a car whose driver has just driven into the back of a bus – in the first and the final analysis computers are controlled by men and women. This simple fact is one which has not been transmitted to the public, indeed the opposite is too often true. We read of computer-controlled underground signalling systems and computer-controlled production lines; of sinister computers that control the world as in '2001'. But the computer is only acting as an intermediary. Its information has been supplied by man, its duties defined by man, and it works at the discretion of man. To assume that a computer runs the underground railway system is as silly as asserting that an 'automatic' car needs no driver. Yet such concepts are fostered by writers and workers in the field and the very language used reinforces the fear of man's being subservient to the machine.

This is not to say that computers are harmless. Like all tools they depend on who uses them and for what purpose, and again we come back to man. This is why we should all be interested, not merely in a quasi-scientific glossy TV magazine way but in a social, political and economic way in what computers do, for whom and why.

If you book a plane ticket with British Airways it is done through a computer-linked system so that any office can locate flights and seats quickly and accurately; the same is true for large theatre booking agencies and the larger hotel groups. The milk in your bottle or carton is measured, tested and indeed gets there through machines which have been programmed to perform these functions with the minimum of human involvement. Your rate demand, pay slip and tax demand are likely to have been processed through a computer. The speed the production line moves at; the buying of raw materials or manufactured intermediate goods, the stocks held, the actual work method, are, in all probability, determined by calculations or information performed by, or stored in, a computer. The goods your local supermarket holds, the shape of your new car, your train schedules, even your toothpaste, all have a computer working somewhere in the process that made or delivered them.

To unscramble all the tax codes, pay slips, insurance premia and policies back to their pre-computer data form would be a Herculean dream, let alone effort. Whereas in the past man's horizons were limited by certain physical capabilities, the computer has, to some extent lifted these limitations. The speed with which calculations and information retrieval can be made has enabled enterprises to expand to sizes greater than was at one time thought to be consistent with efficiency. Management information systems have now pared data dissemination down to its bare bones and may even have arranged that any one manager only receives and only transmits information that is of use to him or his immediate superior. This of course has repercussions on the manager's work content in precisely the same way as tape-controlled machines have a great impact on the craftsmen in, say, engineering. But the impact does not stop there.

Refined information systems standardise the data upon which decisions have to be made. This having been done, not only are standardised decisions capable of being made but, as importantly, an exception to the standard rules is easy to spot and thus centralised compensatory action can be taken at an early stage. This sort of system, impossible without computers, had aided if not encouraged the growth of the conglomerate company, the growth of the multi-national company and finally the growth of the multi-national conglomerate – such as the ITTs of this world. Computers enable analysis to be made much more quickly; thus, economies previously hidden become apparent and reactions to given situations can be made more speedily and with more certainty than before. Thus the computer can claim some responsibility for the phenomenon of 'industrial synergy' which is the 'positive' name for takeovers or asset stripping. The computer is a very potent tool; its potential has been realised by some and exploited by them.

Government, both local and central, becomes increasingly difficult. Industrialised countries are a complex inter-relation of enterprises, in varying degrees of private–public ownership. Each country is related to others through trade and through the third party ownership of multi-national companies. When raw material prices are raised by country A, countries B, C, D and E are affected in varying degrees and this effect has ripple repercussions not only in those countries but on others which neither use, nor produce that raw material. The sheer complexity of the situation has made the use of computers essential. Not only are they used by the Taxation and Social Security agencies but also by Defence, Treasury, Health, Police and Education departments. The advantages are the same as those for private concerns but the disadvantages have wider repercussions. If a computer is programmed wrongly in a private concern the worst that may happen is either a smaller profit for shareholders, some redundancies, or both. Regrettable but at least localised. If a Government computer is programmed wrongly a series of decisions can be made which lead to an extra 1 million unemployed, galloping inflation, or both. 'Programmed wrongly' is also the shorthand way of saying that the wrong assumptions have been made. By blaming the computer or computer operator it is relatively easy for an economist, for example, to save face.

A very interesting programme was shown on television some years ago which neatly showed the advantages and disadvantages of computers. A section of the public, an academic economist and a computer expert set about running the economy. Certain variables were taken into consideration, certain assumptions made and decisions were taken in the light of these. The decisions were fed into a pre-programmed computer and finally the economy was set on an even steady growth path with acceptable levels of inflation and unemployment. The economist then pointed out that other variables existed, variables that were external to the system, i.e., wars, droughts, floods, etc. He showed that the decisions taken by the panel were substantially similar to those taken by successive governments since the war but that these external events had completely ruined forecasts and thus plans. The same external events were then superimposed on the steady growth rate and a totally different picture emerged of incredibly high inflation and an enormous balance of payments deficit.

The lesson is clear. The computer only predicts after being given the facts and if these facts are incomplete the odds are on a totally erroneous forecast. In addition, the right questions have to be asked. Where this problem assumes more sinister proportions is in that because the prediction comes from a computer it is somehow legitimised; computers cannot make mistakes, but unfortunately, men can. Total credence given to computer predictions can be dangerous; even at the simple level of computer-dating, compatibility is only based on variables selected on the questionnaires. Governments must now use computers, but when planning is concerned and the basic data is analysed electronically using man-made models the results must be treated with as large a degree of caution as if they had come from a battery of clerks using quill pens or horoscopes.

Computer is a word that covers a multitude of machines, in the same way that the word 'bird' does not distinguish between an ostrich and a sparrow. There are large computers costing many millions of pounds, small computers costing a mere £20,000; machines which can play chess, others that just store information on magnetic tapes or discs rather like a glorified tape recorder. There are machines to get the best out of machines and machines which work with the basic machines, the basic cake is 'hard-ware' – the icing 'soft-ware'. The hard-ware, however, cannot work without soft-ware and perhaps an apter simile would be that the hard-ware is the operating theatre while the soft-ware includes the scalpels and clamps. Computers may be large machines taking up rooms specially heated and dust-proofed or they may be small filing cabinet-sized machines in an office, or just attached to another machine. They may be operated by one or two people or need many working round the clock in shifts. They may need sophisticated and highly qualified staff or staff with minimal training. They may represent a proportionately high percentage investment or just another small capital outlay. They may store and retrieve information or perform the most complex of mathematical analysis.

Computers not only affect people in their everyday lives as consumers, but affect them at their work-place, both directly and indirectly. Some jobs are lost because of the introduction of computers – a form of technological redundancy. These may be in clerical areas such as filing, secretarial, wages departments, pensions departments, etc., or on the shop-floor where an automated production line or machine tool has replaced manual labour or in the management echelons where new information procedures have bypassed certain people. Indirectly, mergers which could not have taken place but for the computer tend to create redundancies, especially in managerial areas, and computer-based management consultancies have had an unfortunate record in manufacturing redundancies.

Some jobs change. Clerical and administrative staffs no longer have to perform *physically* repetitive tasks; these have been replaced by what are only too often *mentally* repetitive jobs. Craftsmen may be turned into machine-watchers and dial checkers. Some employees may have additional responsibilities, others considerably less. Some may be released to perform tasks for which they have more aptitude, others only stagnate in repetition. Whether these changes are good or bad depends entirely on the individual. One employee may like responsibility, another may not and the view taken of the benefits of the computer will depend on exactly how it has changed the job content with respect to these personal preferences. Old skills may become redundant, new ones may be learned. Whether this is all to the good or not, there is change, and change inevitably brings with it worry, disillusionment and conflict.

On the other hand jobs can be created. It is not unknown for a new data-processing facility to employ 50 per cent as many staff again as the non-computerised section it replaces. The computer manufacturing and servicing industry has become a major employer in its own right. Computer bureaux, on-line services, agencies and consultants using computer facilities all add to the employment field. The credit-card industry could not possibly have expanded at such a furious rate were it not for the computer; the Post Office Giro would not have got off the ground were it not for the computer. Both of these organisations employ many people. Thus in the basic fields of job creation, job content and job destruction computers have had a very considerable impact.

Computers also affect salaries and other conditions of service. If a computer installation makes an enterprise more efficient and thus more profitable it is natural that the employees of that enterprise will seek higher salaries and better conditions of service. This applies not only to the data processing staff but also to the other employees of the enterprise. Salaries for the data processing staff may themselves force up salaries in contiguous areas of the enterprise by distorting the pattern of internal differentials. Shift systems or overtime patterns may be changed after the introduction of computerisation or holidays may have to be taken at fixed periods; conversely the introduction of computerisation may allow for the introduction of flexible working hours and a shorter working week.

What is clear is that computers have a direct or indirect effect on employment and on other bargaining topics. As such the computer has come prominently to the attention of the trade-union movement. Few if any unions are unaffected by computers and few negotiating topics remain outside the influence of computers. Work-people have viewed 'progress' and 'technology' with a somewhat jaundiced eye over the centuries. From the Luddites through the 'Black Cattle' of the South Wales mines and steel works to the present-day runs a common theme of fear. Fear of the unknown, fear of unemployment, and fear for one's children. Although technological change has brought many advantages to the population in general it has wrought a terrible toll in physically and mentally maimed employees. Even in this legislated age deaths from asbestosis and pneumoconiosis are still tolerated, Flixboroughs occur and each day men and women handle chemicals the side effects of which we do not yet know. Successive generations have been told of the wonderful future each advance would bring, yet each time this advance occurred so the crock of gold moved further away. Is it any wonder that employees regard the computer in the same light: as an advance that will bring benefits, but to whom?

Trade unions were founded with, and continue to operate almost entirely on, the contributions of their membership and consequently they have a primary responsibility to represent and protect the interest of that membership. Trade-union members are not only employees, they are also consumers of goods and services, voters, potential patients of the NHS and their families use the education services. Trade unions obviously have the responsibility for matters within the industrial, commercial sector, e.g. collective bargaining, job protection, etc., and they also have a duty to represent these interests and the wider political issues concerning that industry as a whole. In addition to this, trade unions have duties to protect their members, their retired members and the families of both in their other roles as consumers, voters and activists, and this function is increasingly demanded by the membership itself.

Trade unions exist because an individual is at a grave disadvantage when facing an employer. The concept of collectivity is central to trade unionism; it is the only available countervailing power against total domination and subjugation by employers and, in some circumstances, governments. If a trade union is to be successful it must retain its membership and thus its source of income and to do this it must, above all, be seen to be obtaining settlements which are to the satisfaction of the membership. Settlements which embrace the salary package, settlements which protect or improve working prospects, and above all settlements which give its members an adequate standard of living. It is in these contexts that trade unions impinge upon computers and vice versa, because of the large and increasing influence on British life that computers are exerting.

In Britain, new techniques are often viewed with mistrust, as was explained earlier. But the mistrust runs deeper than fear of unknown factors. It is not just with the realms of injury or death that new inventions are associated but more with an increased exploitation of the labour force. In short, if there are two possible assumptions about the motives of a management, relating to almost any management action, employees will automatically assume that the motive is to extend management rights while putting employees at a disadvantage. So it is with computerisation. Employees look for the catch, and it must be admitted that the history of British management and labour relations gives them ample justification for doing so. What makes computers so powerful a talisman is their all-pervasiveness and the range of their functions and potentialities.

It follows that in representing its members a trade union will often come into conflict with the installation or the functions of a computer. It also follows that if the representation is to be effective then the trade-union officers need to have some expertise in the field; this is not to suggest that courses in programming, languages and circuitry should be given to trade-union officials, although there are some data processing consultants and experts who indignantly ask: why not? What an official must be able to do, or at least have access to someone who can do, is to analyse the effects of new installations on all the factors that may affect the employees' lives. This is, of course, not as easy as it sounds because the main source of interpretation is the employer, and no-one can deny that he has a vested interest in presenting data in a light most favourable to himself. As if this did not make life difficult enough there are many occasions when the employer himself cannot predict the total effect of introducing a computer or computerised process.

It must be admitted that the British trade-union movement has not been conspicuously successful in its dealings with the situation. Far too often both members and officials have allowed themselves to be spellbound by the jargon (in much the same way that employers fell before the computer salesmen in the 1960s). Rather than admit ignorance of the subject and ask for really detailed explanations, vague generalisations have been allowed to slip by without challenge, something that would not have happened in other negotiating or consultative areas. Some unfortunate consequences have arisen from this, not the least important being the 'once bitten – twice shy' syndrome; trade unions have become determined that such bamboozling will never occur again.

Nevertheless trade unions are consumers of the computer's services. Some trade unions have their own installation, some use bureaux, some share. This use is basically administrative but it could and probably will expand into research and, with impending legislation, economic and commercial forecasting.

There are many other issues which directly affect trade unions in their normal work which bring them face to face with computers. Productivity schemes, job evaluation proposals and bonus schemes, are now usually calculated or predicted on computers and unless the union is prepared to become a mere information receiver it must be able to check the data presented to it. This is of course most important and has associated with it the fundamental question of data verification and acceptance in all situations. Personnel files, health files, potential black-listing, fidelity bonds are all, if not products of the computer, at least considerably facilitated by the computer. The problem for the unions is that abuse of the information stored or simple mistakes in preparation of the data, can have far-reaching employment consequences for individuals, even to the extent of following them throughout a working lifetime.

The clock cannot be turned back. Technological change, whether for good or evil, continues apace, most of it using computers in the process of invention or application. Advances in medicine, space exploration, raw material exploitation, modes of travel, food technology are all vital to mankind in a world of fixed finite resources and the computer is a valuable tool in such research. In industry and commerce the computer can lead to increased efficiency and the saving of manpower, which if passed on to the consumer should result in lower or stabilised prices. As a force for good the computer offers enormous potential.

On the other side of the coin the computer offers scope for the surveillance and control of populations at large. Research on and the development of weapons of destruction are made that much easier and more efficient. Technological unemployment and underemployment have been created. Profits have been boosted but wages and salaries have not increased proportionately, as a result of increased productivity. New plant has become more capital-intensive yet no method has been found to absorb those who would have been employed or to provide leisure activities for the increased leisure hours now available.

The trade-union movement has tended, by and large, to react to given sets of circumstances rather than initiating new action. As a result unions have been on the defensive in that they have had to cope with the difficulties produced after the installation of a computer. Fortunately, this attitude is now changing and the more forward-looking trade unions are insisting upon prior consultation before changes in work methods and work loads actually take place. This in itself is a great step forward because it will remove a great deal of the fear and suspicion surrounding the computer. The days were when the employees had a briefing from a computer consultant who, instead of telling them how an installation was going to affect their jobs, went into a long diatribe on the potential efficiency benefits of the installation peppered with words like 'interface', 'hard-ware', 'soft-ware', the odd 'digital', frequent 'binaries' and references to 'inputs', 'facsimile transmissions' and 'critical analyses'. To most of the employees present the talks might as well have been presented in Martian. The real offence was that this method of presentation was the only source of information many employees received; it was an exercise in mystification rather than illumination; at times, one would suspect, deliberately so. Trade union insistence upon consultations before the event has now precluded this form of dialogue.

As business concentration increases through mergers and takeovers, as governments intervene more into everyday affairs, so both computers and trade unions will have increasingly important roles to play. The one as the vehicle of providing the methods by which such operations will become feasible, the other as the counterbalance to the increasing remoteness and the increasing strength of those who are in control. Confrontation is not the method of choice although it cannot be denied that at times there may be conflicts of interest. The challenge is for the trade-union movement to harness the computer for its own use and for the benefit of its members as a whole.

Chapter 2

The computers about us

Computers do not exist in a vacuum in Britain, they are part of a complex industrialised society, existing alongside other pieces of machinery, either man-made or consisting of men and women. In economic terms Britain has a mixed economy of both public and private enterprises, in social terms it is still remarkably class- and status-ridden and in personnel terms shows a marked inequality in the distribution of wealth, although less so in incomes. The complexity stems from the inter-relation of the different sectors of the economy, from their international linkages, from the impact of government, and now EEC, decisions on all forms of enterprises and from the social and regional structures. Describing such an economy in detail is thankfully not a task of this book; indeed many eminent commentators have differed so radically on such a description that one comes to believe that perhaps it is a futile task in any event. However, we do need some simple breakdown of the system in order to separate out the impact that computers can have on unions, and on lives and so it will be divided into the very broad sectors of manufacturing, distribution, services and government.

Having had the temerity to sectionalise the economy it must also be admitted that the computer has a rather complex set of applications which themselves need classifying. Not only do computers differ in size, price, range and sophistication but they also differ in the way they are used and the manner in which they relate to the organisation which is making use of them. In broad terms again these will be described as 'in-house' installations, bureaux, and time-sharing.

It is most misleading to write of the computer as though it was some single entity like a person. It is more like writing about football with international sides, first-division sides, fourth-division sides and non-league sides all of which have the same right to be called football teams even though everyone realises the disparities in resources and talent. Even within the three main heads described above there are important differences in installation. Some are large, very sophisticated machines, costing literally £5 million for the basic machines and another £1 million for all the additional trimmings, others cost £20,000 and are self-contained little units performing a known, limited, number of functions. Some machines, like the airlines' booking system, are called 'real-time' with viewing screens showing answers to questions almost immediately or on the push of several buttons. 'Real-time' is a more modern innovation and represents the computer adjusting its information out, as information is fed into it. In everyday usage it tends to represent the everyday conception of the computer. Others have the different function of printing out invoices or relaying notifications. Others are capable of doing the arithmetic for very complex mathematical operations in seconds and others can produce three-dimensional drawings on viewing screens. In some cases, such as the Prudential Assurance Company, the head office installation requires a full-time staff of 560 – some of whom are highly qualified – while at the other end of the scale a mini-computer may require only three people – none of whom need more training than the average GPO-trained switchboard operator.

The 'in-house' installation is normally the largest operation and means that the enterprise has its own computer. In the late 1960s there was a rush by large companies either to buy or lease their own equipment, often regardless of cost and unfortunately regardless of need. The large computer was going to solve all of Britain's problems and there was a frantic scamper to acquire it, often for the worst of motives: that of keeping up with the Jones's. There was a lack of adequately trained personnel and an absence of reliability in the machines themselves. Additional expenses which had not been foreseen by the buyer mounted as necessary adjustments had to be purchased and in 1971 the whole edifice tumbled. A general economic recession had violent effects on the computer industry. New orders were cancelled as enterprises took a hard look at their costs and started to retrench. Surplus staff were shed and an effort made to utilise the startlingly high level of spare computer capacity. Unions had problems as well as companies.

However, once an enterprise had acquired an expensive installation it was difficult to get rid of it. Systems of data collection, expensive in themselves, had been set up and tailored to the requirements of the computer and few if any boards of directors were willing to write off the large capital cost because if they did so they would have been seen to have made a mistake in the first place. Installations stayed, staffs were pared down, proper objectives established, proper staff training undertaken and slowly data-processing departments began to breath again. However, the large in-house installations are now working at less than 50 per cent of their capacity on average across Britain (according to figures given by the Data Processing Managers Association), a legacy from the more extravagant days when even the smallest enterprises had to have their own computer and their quota of graduate managers.

In-house, however, means not only having a head office installation. There can be a series of linked computers as at the British Steel Corporation or there can be 'on-line' terminals in various plants or branch offices. 'On-line terminals' means that an operator can either call for information, or feed information into, the central installation. Nowadays the tendency is to lease rather than purchase a new computer. This is because the capital cost is very high and if a computer is leased servicing is that much more efficient, rather as in the case of renting instead of buying a colour TV set.

The other reason is that computers tend to become obsolescent rather more quickly than most other machines and that especially applies to the peripheral 'soft-ware' that goes with the main installation. One has only to look at the second-hand machines being offered by dealers to realise that either obsolescence or enterprises moving away from data-processing must be increasing at a rather fast rate.

Bureaux are exactly what they sound. They offer a service to potential clients in the form of a pre-prepared package upon which the various elements of the clients' requirements are superimposed. A bureaux service has one great advantage for the smaller or even small enterprise in that it incurs no capital outlay, only an ongoing cost which can be met from current revenue. Even larger companies have switched, or are thinking of switching, to bureaux. Generally the service offered is simple, reflecting a costly, time consuming job such as pay-rolling or invoicing, although some do offer far more sophisticated services. The problem for the potential user is to know which bureaux can deliver which services and, more to the point, which can deliver what they promise.

In the pre-1971 computer boom bureaux sprung up overnight as whiz-kids with knowledge of one or two basic programs set about leasing second-hand equipment and started with two or three staff. This form of uncontrolled growth stopped with the crash but too late to rescue the good name of bureaux in general. Clients whose problems did not quite fit the programs often either had to alter their methods of data collection at great expense or were left badly in the lurch; small bureaux could not deliver to time when one or two of the staff went sick or went on holiday. Around 1971 at least half the bureaux disappeared, leaving the larger more stable ones with some capital and steady income, to dominate the market although there has been a trend from 1975 for this field to expand partly due to the leasing policies of the computer manufacturers and partly to the unused capacity abounding in large installations.

Bureaux, like computers themselves, vary greatly in size, type, machinery used, ownership and competence. The *Computer Users' Year-book 1975* lists 214 different bureaux in the United Kingdom. Others existed which it was thought did not have all the necessary specifications for inclusion in the reference book. Some of the bureaux are either departments of, or subsidiaries of, computer manufacturing companies, others are large company 'in-house' installations with obviously much spare capacity such as Unilever. London University's computer is represented as is the Post Office with its National Data Processing Service. Others are bureaux which also offer consultancy and programming services while yet others are basically bureaux only. One bureau even has IBM computers in the USA using satellite transmissions. To add complexity to an already complicated situation computer bureaux can offer very fast or somewhat slower (batch) services; they can offer their own terminals – a method of nominating information and getting results directly from the computer – (there were eighty-six of these in 1975), or operate a postal or telegram or messenger service. The price paid for the service not unnaturally reflects the sophistication and speed of the service offered. There are, of course, drawbacks for users. One is a constant worry about security and although this is not to say that bureaux are any less secure than in-house installations, it reflects that feeling of 'it is out of our hands and we are dependent . . . '. Reliability-lapses due to extraneous factors such as power losses (and no standby generator) also add to corporate worries. Worries notwithstanding, the bureaux are burgeoning and since in commerce and industry there is scarcely a single production or service process without anxieties, in this sense computer bureaux fit neatly into Britain's business life.

The third method of computer usage is time-sharing. In some degree this has been covered by the bureaux – indeed some of them offer time-sharing as a sole service. However, it is different in essence. There are few if any services offered other than time on an under-utilised set of equipment by a genuine time-sharing concern. Users generally need quite sophisticated problems solved, and solved quickly and so use the available machinery.

As an adjunct to all three types of usage an industry of program writing and consultancy has sprung up to advise, cajole, flatter and generally service users and potential users. Again this shows how closely the brave new world of computers has followed the traditional patterns of British service industries: its separation from the mainstreams is now by specialisation and jargon alone.

The users of these services come from all the sectors of British and, on occasion, international life; private and public, educational and military, health and research. Each enterprise or department decides upon computer usage because in the judgement of their managements it will enhance whatever is their function. This may be a service or it may be a product, it may be to increase profits or to provide a social service. The computer may be capable of making some processes more efficient by increasing the speed of production, it may increase profits by cutting costs, simplify a tax collection system, help run a hospital efficiently, aid operations on the stock exchange or check football pools more quickly. In all cases managements believed or still believe that the computer would help them solve problems with which they were confronted. Too often managers forgot that employees were involved in these processes, or would be involved in the procedures and thus forgot, indeed still forget, to consult, inform and even take advice on what to do in relation to their work force in the new circumstances. It is in these situations that a trade union has to react to defend its members and it is these self-same circumstances which have given the computer such a dubious reputation among workers the length and breadth of Britain.

The in-house installation has been the main stimulus for such personnel mis-management. Managements have often allowed rumours of impending redundancies among clerical staff to go unchallenged, sometimes because some of these rumours were true but at other times because of sheer incompetence. In-house installations are normally (though not always) large and if the equipment is moved into the same building as the other head office staffs it is hardly likely to go unnoticed yet it is often these staffs whose jobs will change the most with the arrival of such an installation. On occasion the computer is placed in a separate building and only rumours filtering back, often distorted, allow staff to know initially of its existence. If it does nothing else a computer will be used to make-up the payroll and thus the wages department will often be wary about the security of their jobs; an invoice department will have the same worries. But there are other fears. Many jobs, both in these departments and in other spheres encompassing management, supervision, manual worker and skilled crafts could be made redundant by an installation or their job contents could change markedly.

It has been estimated that 47 per cent of all computer staffs work in in-house installations for large companies and this statistic at least gives an indication of the scope of this particular problem. Changes in job content and responsibilities can be most disrupting when a career has been established or mapped out on the assumption that existing skills are adequate and necessary. Obviously, for many employees, the older they are, the longer in that job or industry they have been, the more difficult it becomes to adapt to change. Yet change is what the computer brings. Clerical skills are the first to suffer. Wages and invoice clerks spring readily to mind because they are universal to almost all computer users yet the specialist clerical jobs in the specialist concerns like shipping, insurance, banking, broking, may all have their singular talents changed out of all recognition. These changes have had an unfortunate tendency to make the majority of jobs more repetitive and boring although a minority have become more interesting with increased responsibility and scope. In some concerns the introduction of an in-house installation has led management to offer posts in the new department to existing staffs who would otherwise be redundant, after, and conditional upon, suitability after training. Such managements have also proved to be the exception rather than the rule.

In-house installation can also affect managerial responsibilities very greatly, especially if the installation is of the type where there are terminals in branches or plants and a two-way information flow, or a one-way instruction flow develops. Information may be rationed, targets may be set by those with little knowledge of the production problems, particularly in conglomerate companies, with decisions being made by those who are one or two higher up the managerial pyramid. At the other end of the scale, production of other work schedules such as those of a salesman's or driver's can change as the enterprise seeks to make optimum use of its resources. Unfortunately again the management only realise after the event that such use not only depends on the cooperation of those human resources but that the resources themselves are often not the same when working involves the new conditions.

A further complication of in-house methods is that a totally new department is grafted onto what is probably a long-established structure. This can lead to jealousies and inequities especially when salary negotiations are not conducted by collective bargaining. Matters are not helped by the Electronic Data Processing (EDP) department generally being cut off from the main stream of company activities, both socially or on a business level, sometimes for geographical economy reasons but at other times by the jargon used and the totally different jobs they are doing. We shall return to this in more detail in a later chapter but even where collective bargaining takes place the danger is that the EDP department may be seen to receive special treatment which in turn creates dissension and disillusionment within the computer structure. The job itself may make for suspicion of the personnel in the department because the effects of the installation are perceived to be directly due to the new personnel; for example new and stringent working conditions to improve overall productivity often stem from the productivity of the computer staff themselves. Such staff are then regarded as a tool of management, or as an extension of the mechanical installation itself.

Neither bureaux usage nor time-sharing attracts the same problems, although the effect on the non-EDP employees may be precisely the same. Because the number of EDP staff is so much smaller for the average user (if there are any at all) and because the bulk of the work is done on service contract basis well removed from the users' personnel, potential conflicts rarely come to the surface. Somehow, it is rather like the difference between killing someone with a bayonet and killing people by bombing them; 'because you don't see it you can bomb it' becomes more easily acceptable.

There are of course, occasions and situations where a computer installation has little or no effect on the number of jobs or the job content of other employees. University research departments are one such, although the research functions and skills have had to change somewhat to keep abreast of the new techniques in data-processing.

Computer users are from all of the four basic sectors of the economy that we outlined above, that is the manufacturing, service, distribution and government sectors. Within each of these there are the sub-divisions and classes of sub-divisions which together give a totality of life in Britain because the computer and its products are now affecting almost the sum total of national activities. The computer has had an effect on the working lives of employees in all of the sub-divisions, varying in degree and type depending on the type of work done, and the goods or services offered, so that in order to look at this impact we must first break down this specification into a more detailed form.

The scope of the problem is immense. There are allegedly between 22 and 24 million men and women in the economically active work-force; the problems of precise numbering are formidable because some workers (predominantly married women) drift into and out of the labour market, the number of pensioners of all descriptions who still work and the unknown number of people doing more than one paid job. According to the *Computer Users' Yearbook 1975*, there are 9,300 machines in 5,450 departments and this is not an exclusive list. This would mean that for every one machine there are approximately 2,760 employees, and this is only the size of a medium-sized industrial company, in other words we have a high ratio EDP society.

The British economy is a very integrated one and in the private sector a very concentrated one too. The top 100 companies control 50 per cent of output in money terms and these companies typically tend to be multi-plant, multi-product, and multi-national. It will be argued later in this book that the computer aided, and in some instances, inspired this concentration. Taking each sector individually it will be possible to see where the computer fits in and roughly what it is used for.

Britain built its industrial revolution in the late eighteenth and nineteenth centuries on the switch from agricultural work to manufacturing. It combined the resulting cheap labour with new technologies and a policy of importing foodstuffs from the Empire and exporting finished manufactured goods to the world. Traditionally in the modern era Britain has thus been a manufacturing country. To get the best returns from industry natural resources such as coal and iron were used and will be included in this manufacturing sector, which tragically, both in terms of manpower employed and percentage of Gross Domestic Product is declining. Tragically, because many reputable analysts of all political persuasions feel that this is the root cause of our current industrial and economic problems. The manufacturing sector tends typically to be dominated by a few large producers in each product range or what the economists call an oligopolistic situation. For example there are only four mass-consumption car producers, three producers of detergents and two large producers of glass. On the other hand there are still industries which are made up of a myriad of small firms – as in the boot and shoe or clothing industries – none of which can dominate the market.

In the public sector some companies, notably the British Steel Corporation, Rolls-Royce (1971), British Petroleum and British Leyland compete directly with other privately-owned companies in the same industry. Most of the large manufacturing firms have computers somewhere either with large 'in-house' installations – like Ford, BLMC, Shell, BSC, etc. – or by using the bureaux for salaries. Basically, the larger the company the more it will use and rely on the computer or even a series of computers. Not only can computers aid salary and employee-benefit computations but also change or enhance, in three basic forms, the productive processes used by the companies.

The first is the control of track speeds depending on fixed output targets which have themselves probably been set by using a computer. The second is the actual machinery used. This involves mainly the numerically controlled machines, typically lathes or welding machines, although computer-run steel plants are now becoming run of the mill. The third is the coordination of production between different plants and different products to get what is considered to be the optimum output. In the case of a multi-national organisation this may be the optimum on a global not national scale. Each of these uses plus the use of computers in product research, development and design, has work implications for the employees of the enterprise and possibly also for employees of enterprises which supply goods to or receive products from the users. All types of employees on the production side will be affected, whether manual, technical, scientific, craft or managerial; while in the non-production areas of a manufacturing firm stock-control procedures and clerical procedural changes will affect these employees too. As there has been a steady drift within manufacturing companies from the direct production employee to the indirect support staff in total percentage terms the latter effects are becoming more important. The manufacturing sector includes of course, the computer manufacturers themselves.

The second sector in which computers operate is in the service fields. Services vary as much as manufactured products can vary; from hairdressing to health, from gambling to insurance. This sector is large and growing in Britain. Banking, insurance companies and credit houses all use the computer to a great extent to clear cheques, record policies and check creditworthiness. But there are of course, far more services than just these three which use the computer. Theatre bookings are now made on central computers, airline bookings the same, some betting-shop organisations use them, newspapers, books and magazines all use the services of the computer somewhere between the inception of the idea and the finished product reaching the consumer. The Post Office makes great use of computers and indeed runs its own computer bureaux and agency; the Stock Exchange now has a rival in the Ariel computer system and the Exchange itself is becoming computerised. Personal motoring can even be affected by computer-linked traffic lights, although many of us believe that these are calculated to drive the private motorist from the road.

Services tend to use more real-time machinery because there is more direct dealing with the public and this type of operation is ideal for this type of use. A flick or two of the fingers and a query can be solved without reference to record books or phone-calls which appear to take forever – furthermore the result is more likely to be correct. Employees similarly tend to use more real-time machinery, but it should be recognised that in some cases there are areas of quite heavy conflict. For example, in newspapers or magazine production there is a very strong resistance from the print unions to automated systems. On the other side of this coin this is the sector in which computer application can actually create jobs as in the credit card or Giro systems. Other jobs have changed as techniques have changed, notably in seat booking and in insurance and banking.

The third sector is distribution. Britain led the world to the industrial revolution and thus had to lead the world in the distribution of the manufactured products, hence our early development of railways. The distributive industries include rail, road haulage, shipping and docks, and civil air transport, although one can also include wholesaling and warehousing (not in the Stock Exchange sense), and commodity marketing as well as retail sales outlets whether by post or in stores. There have been large changes in this sector during the last decade, many of which have come about as an indirect result of computerisation. For example, the growth in containerisation and the consequent linkages needed between rail, sea, and road transport to determine the movements of each has needed computer application on an international as well as a national scale. The gradual change from the corner shop to the chain supermarket has been greatly aided by computers doing the stock controlling of the chain. British Rail use computers in signalling, marshalling yards and the Post Office is slowly becoming more automated.

Distribution is in a sense a very underdeveloped sector. Each of the operators has operated independently, often in wasteful competition with the other and it is only now, when fuel costs have made us aware of energy conservation that there has been any movement towards integration of the services. Indeed, the opposite has been true. Rail-lines were closed, cutting off producers from this method of carriage but no roads were built to enable the bulk-carrying to be continued by lorry; canals have been neglected and remarkably under-used. The energy crisis has stimulated thoughts of a national distribution plan and should this occur the computer will be the mainstay in coordinating all the different forms of traffic.

The final sector is the Government sector including both local and central government and the non-crown Civil Service agencies. This sector has been growing in manpower terms, growing in general economic terms and growing in computer-use terms. As government has become more complex, often as a result of national and international inter-relations rather than conscious political decisions, so the need for computers has expanded. Central government departments need to store and then to be able to retrieve information speedily and accurately, so that their statistical series can be presented while medium- and long-term trends can be monitored. Computers also have payroll and accounting functions, and are used for problem solving and model testing. Although each department has responsibility for its own installations (there are over 200 of them) there is also a Government Central Computer Agency with personnel in each of the departments.

Government agencies also use computers. The Manpower Services Commission is aiming to have a complete network of computer-linked Jobcentres and has made a start in this direction; the Vehicle Licensing Centre in Swansea is fully computerised although at enormous cost over-runs. Each university maintains its own installation which is used for teaching computer technology as well as being available for all forms of research and doing the usual basic payrolls, etc. In some of the more technologically oriented universities these installations can be extremely large.

Local government is also a big user of computers and local government reorganisation proved to be a boon to the computer manufacturers as larger installations were needed to deal with the larger new units. The same system of new ordering is now starting to apply to the National Health Service following reorganisation and the creation of the very large Regional Health Authorities. Health records can be traced more easily, and the computer should make the study of epidemiology (the distribution of diseases) that much easier and consequently benefit the public in the years ahead. Rates and taxes may be unpopular but in the last analysis an industrial nation cannot exist without them and if the computer makes loopholes hard to exploit and gets a higher percentage yield then it is fulfilling a useful purpose.

These are the basic types of computer usage and the very broad areas in which computers are used. The over-riding point is that no sector is an island unto itself; it is inextricably linked to the other sectors and one major problem of computer-use is that when one organisation takes a decision based on its computations it cannot fully or accurately predict the effect this will have on other parts of the economy. We shall deal with this problem later in the book.

Chapter 3

Computers, people and jobs

The decades of the 1950s and 1960s and the first two years of the 1970s were ones of uncritical acceptance of the dogma 'big is good'. These years saw a marked growth in the size of companies, a surge in mergers and takeovers, the birth of the asset stripper and the more legitimate conglomerate. The multi-national corporation spread like giant hog-weed; government ministries were coalesced into vast departments; local government and the Health Services were reorganised on a large unit basis and the ultimate in large scale, the Common Market, was called forth. These two decades saw changes which, in their less publicised way, have had, and will continue to have effects on the world population as far reaching as the original industrial revolution itself.

This move to greatness (or grossness) in all sectors and the transcending of frontiers was aided by, indeed made possible by, the computer. All people are affected, from children at school, non-work-force housewives, all forms of employees, pensioners, to the sick and the disabled. Because of this incredibly wide impact it was inevitable that trade unions would become intimately involved, even if the involvement was provoked by the resulting symptoms rather than the computer itself.

However, there has been a subtle change in attitude over the last few years. Criticism is being levelled at the philosophy of 'big is good' on moral, philosophical, political and economic grounds and although it is not the purpose of this chapter to explore the implications of this change in attitude it will be examined later. The change is exemplified by the clamour for political devolution, the small workers' cooperative and, closer to home, the switch of users from the large to the mini-computer. What, however, this chapter does deal with is Britain as it is at present where large units prevail in all the sectors described in Chapter 2. We shall look at these sectors in greater detail with particular emphasis on the jobs and functions involved.

The manufacturing industries in Britain, both public and private still employ 34.5 per cent of the working population. Although we no longer produce the same range of goods as we did in the late 1960s, the spectrum is still impressive; although as we import more, so our range declines and capacity is lost. The computer is well entrenched in almost all enterprises even if there is just a basic bought-in bureaux service, but often the computer has far more wide-ranging effects on work and production methods, on output and on control.

With the concept of the remuneration package, involving as it does elements which cost the employer monies but which can involve a wide variety of benefits, most companies employing over 250 people have had to turn to the computer to record and work out this remuneration in bills and payments. Taxation policies, their frequent changes and the introduction of earnings-related National Insurance payments have reinforced this trend. The large concerns use their own installations for this purpose, the smaller ones use bureaux.

The size of the 'in-house' installation will vary depending on quite what is required of it, and the size and qualifications of staff will depend on the machines used. The mini-computer with one or two basic programs written by an agency is capable of handling medium-sized companies' payrolls, records and invoices, but its size of course limits the amount that can be stored in it although its working lifetime should be considerable providing the organisation does not grow out of the installation. An attraction of the larger mini-computer is that there is little need to have many qualified new staff, indeed the salesman of the machines point out that existing clerical staff can be retrained. What they do not point out is the cost of altering existing data-collection methods. The mini-computer is selling well at present, partly due to the prevailing economic stringencies, its comparatively low cost, and partly due to the fact that enterprises still like the status of having their own in-house installation but have realised that the large machines will leave them with a burden of unused capacity.

A mini-computer can run 'on-line' with terminals in branch offices or it can be a single installation alone. It is unlikely to occupy the full-time attention of more than three people and terminals can be operated easily by one person. It can, however, perform many service tasks such as invoicing, stock-controlling, pensions and payrolling more than adequately for a small company or enterprise and store records for others. It tends to have only a clerical work impact in a direct sense as its installation can lead to redundancies in the clerical areas. For those who stay and are retrained to operate the machine there is little difference in job content in that both sets of jobs (wages clerks or mini-computer operators) have limited responsibilities and require a limited, if specific, set of skills. Indirectly it can affect information collection in the enterprise and thus line-managers' or supervisors' work content in some degree.

The larger computers, whether in-house or externally used through time-sharing or a bureau can, and often do, have a significantly greater impact on people's work. There is the first impact of the EDP department on the other staffs working for the company. In the manufacturing sector a company that can afford, or needs to use, a larger computer is probably multi-product and almost certainly multi-plant. Whether or not such a company would have a single central installation or a series of divisionally-based ones will depend on the size of the divisions and the corporate strategy of the company in general and these vary immensely. For example, GEC claims to be a particularly decentralised operation while

Ford is highly centralised; British Leyland is, at present, very decentralised, while IBM is very centralised. The difference in computer terms is that a single head office department will be very large, employ a large number of staff – up to 500 – and this will have a direct impact on that head office staffing, but limited to that one location alone. It is probable that many of the previously employed wages, invoice, billing and stock clerks will still be employed to tabulate and check information and some of them will be trained to put it into an acceptable form for the installation.

Grafted onto this layer will be the technical data-processing people, the operators, programmers, analysts, managers, service staff, etc., who will know little if anything about the company's business and who unfortunately have, historically, not attempted to rectify the situation. If the total computer installation is spread around the various divisions and plants of the company, each of which has its own staff, the ultimate problem, though repeated, will be smaller and less acute. It would appear that it is not so much the ratio of data-processing staff to other staff but the sheer size of the staff which is important in the context of inter-departmental friction.

There were 7,705,000 employees in the British manufacturing industries in 1974 and of these an increasing number are defined as being on staff or 'white collar'. It is probable that nearly all of them are affected by a computer installation except for typists/secretaries though even here the use of automated office machinery is encroaching on their domain. The change in work techniques has been towards the simple, repetitive technical job, card punching, etc., and towards the use of standardised statistical bases. This implies two things. The first is that as the education system in Britain by and large lags well behind technology, there has to be a concerted effort to provide in-job or release-type training. The second is that the area of individual idiosyncracies has been diminished and anomalies and problems, once the interesting part of a clerk's work, have either been abolished, or, when they do happen, are merely irritants.

It is not only the clerical sector that is affected, however, it is the productive process itself. Computers not only provide the services to a manufacturing company but also have a strong operational function in two areas, corporate and on the shop-floor directly, while the corporate effect also effects the plant indirectly. A multi-plant, multi-product company such as Courtaulds, Unilever, or ICI will attempt to equalise the returns from its various divisions and plants, attempt to optimise its returns on all plants and attempt to coordinate its outputs and use of materials especially where they are intra-company trading. This leads to an extremely complex set of arithmetical calculations and although these are theoretically possible without a computer they are unlikely to be possible practically given the scale of the calculations and the time needed to do them manually.

The management accounting use of the computer often starts accidentally. Data called for from managers can be standardised and when exceptions occur they stand out markedly from the rest, and when spotted it is easy to take the appropriate steps to enforce uniformity. Consultants using computer-based techniques flourished in the 1960s and early 1970s but have since fallen on slightly harder times. One good reason for this is that computers can only analyse, and then only on the basis of data fed into them. They can be programmed to spot an anomaly and to analyse all the statistics and emerge with the relevant correlations (and irrelevant correlations), they can multiply or regress anything or everything but they rely completely on the validity and accuracy of the data fed in. This raises several basic points which can be looked at in principle, although the details will follow in the course of this book.

The approximation problem is a real one; in economics it is known as the aggregation problem and judging combined. Although forms can be designed to get standard information, the information itself may be incapable of standardisation; rather than scrap the whole project an approximation is taken. This would be fine if all the data was treated in the same way and in the same direction (then the appropriate corrections can be made) but unfortunately this is not done for much of the time. This leads to errors of unknown magnitude and direction in the aggregates. Along comes a computer, does all the sums perfectly, somehow legitimising the result and the managers who have to take decisions on given information take them on inaccurate predictions.

The second problem is two-fold. What information do you collect and how do you treat the circumstances behind a series of statistics? Sins of omission are prevalent. The factors involved in production may well depend shall we say, on the occupation of the Spanish Sahara affecting phosphate prices and deliveries, yet the probability of such an occupation is not generally written into a computer program. This externality problem is important the reverse way round when a process is geared to the high prices prevalent due to a national catastrophe or war but these prices will fall by an unknown in the future. All the costings are based on the past known facts – intuition, although valuable, has to be dropped. Another view of this is in the social sense. What company programs its computer to take into account the local social and environmental problems that may be caused by a new productive process? Few, if any, because even if the social will and conscience were present, most of the effects are non-quantifiable in computer programming terms. Yet again if production has fallen, is the health of the work-force ever used as a variable, indeed is the health of the work-force ever correlated against the factors used in the productive process itself? If it was done, and this surely is one use to which the spare capacity of so many of the British installations could surely be put, it would be very much in the employees' interests. Cynically, one might suggest that is the reason it is never done.

Corporate strategies based on such information can act as a guide, nothing more, yet to justify both the capital outlay and the running costs or fees, managements are often forced into the position of treating them as more than this, in fact, treating them as facts divinely delivered. People's jobs are at stake, people's job satisfaction and health are at risk as well as corporate profits. In this sector of the economy with a diminishing number of jobs, diminishing investment and disappearing profits, something seems to have gone wrong. It can partially be explained by the use to which the computer is put.

If companies wish to maximise profits, or maximise sales as all the economics and business administration courses tell you they do, it often entails changes in the method of production. Production line speeds are increased and fewer employees produce more goods. It is unusual to find such a process an uplifting one for the employees who remain. The Organisation and Methods man with his stopwatch and measuring tape is a familiar sight in Britain measuring inches rather than yards, millimetres rather than metres and timing in seconds rather than minutes. The O & M people now have computers to back them up and analyse their findings and computations and this quickly enables them to define the optimum positioning to minimise hand, body and feet movements for the performance of industrial tasks and even for the calculations of the time spent walking to the lavatories and the average time spent in them.

What cannot be taken into consideration is how employees are feeling, a pregnant woman, or a man with prostate problems will have more frequent trips and spend longer in a lavatory, people with varicose veins will need to move their legs more and so on. The British people dislike being regimented, there is still a regard for the eccentric and this extends to a rather jaundiced view of authority itself. If a system is produced from the O & M and data-processing department without the reason being explained to those who have to work it (and this is commonplace) it is unreasonable to expect the British to operate it seriously. What is even more to the point is that additional pressures are applied to employees who generally get little increased benefit to compensate for them.

The problem takes a more serious form when new track speeds are introduced; it is remarkable how they seem never to be reduced. Critical Path Analysis can certainly eliminate wasted time but when this is combined with increased production targets and faster conveyor belt speeds it takes no regard of the employees' reactions. Production line working is by common consent a boring occupation, often carried on in the most unpleasant of environments. All data-processing staff should really work on a line for a lengthy period, if they are working for a company which employs these techniques, to appreciate the difficulties caused by some of their outputs. Increasing speeds can only work if employees are feeling well and on top of the job all the time but patently this is nonsense. We all have days when we are feeling, as the patent nostrum peddlers allege, several degrees under. In an office or in most jobs this does not matter, we all walk, have a talk, look out of a window and relax while looking busy. This cannot be done on a production line. If the job is to put in six rivets they have to be put in while the line is passing and the result of higher track speeds, but the same number of employees, is generally a higher percentage of faulty products.

This is not to argue that there can be no improvement in productivity in Britain. There is immense room for improvement but it cannot be imposed; employees have a right to know why it is being done, for whom it is being done and a right to be consulted before the new methods are put into operation. The computer has, because of the increased scope it gives analysts and consultants, played its part in many such changes in Britain but overall our productivity per employee is still low when compared with other industrial economies. This is partly due to the obsolete capital equipment currently in use in Britain, but it is also due to the fact that little attempt has been made to explain the changes to those who will be most affected – the production workers themselves. Obviously the trade unions should be brought in at the analytical or data-collecting stage and a dialogue should ensue up to, and indeed after, the implementation stage; employees will not believe an employer on matters of this sort and history supports their scepticism.

Another area of production influenced by automation is with the numerically controlled machine (NCM). Where in the past craftsmen were skilled and (although it is now almost a cliché) took pride in their work, the growth of these machines has removed the need for skills and the reason for pride except in cases of machine breakdown. An NCM is one which works on instructions fed into it, generally on tape rather like the old pianola. Once Napoleon derisively called us 'a nation of shopkeepers' (he didn't say what the French themselves were) but now we are in danger of becoming a nation of machine-watchers. The craft unions have, by and large, managed to ensure that all machines are minded by a skilled craftsman but the speed at which an NCM can produce a product is many times greater than the individual craftsman could ever manage so that unless productivity exceeds that multiple the number of craftsmen needed will diminish and among other things the union will lose membership. It is of course, an increase in efficiency but the structure of the British economy does not allow for the human problems thus caused and we shall return to this problem later.

Finally in the production sector itself there is the virtually automated plant. Steel, nuclear power, and other capital intensive industries such as petro-chemicals are starting to use these methods. Strip-steel rolling and pickling lines can now be manned by five or six employees where once there were 200. For the few still there the jobs are more interesting, have more responsibility and are far cleaner and far less dangerous than they were before the computerised techniques. This is the promise of the computer! But as with the numerically controlled machine what happened to the other 194 employees?

In the manufacturing sector computers are also used in Research and Development, in cost accounting, in stock analysis and in information dissemination. We have concentrated on shop-floor and clerical employees' implications but computers have an effect on the roles of supervisory and managerial staffs too. One can see the day, and not too distant at that, when a foreman at a large plant will have to be conversant with computer techniques and no longer will there be promotion upwards from the shop-floor, rather graduates or similarly qualified people will take the supervisory jobs. As this will cut off many people from promotion the social implications of this change are frightening. Information rationing affects management, especially line management situations away from the decision-making process, and this combined with strict targeting, restricts the managerial prerogative so beloved (but often so misapplied) of the British management today.

The service sector has different uses for and thus different problems with the computer. There are no production schedules to be changed, nor are there track speeds to be increased or decreased, although there is production in the sense that a service employer will be as keen to increase the number of clients satisfied, with the same or fewer number of staff, as any manufacturing sector employer who wishes to increase output.

As has been said previously, the computer is now vital to the day-to-day running of the large insurance companies, the banks, building societies, betting shops, airlines and a host of other smaller industries. Naturally salaries, pensions and accounting are controlled by the computer but the uses to which the computer is put are far more wide-ranging. Insurance companies can, at the flick of several switches, record policies and thus monitor cash flows in against possible liabilities and can arrange for maturing policies automatically to be presented on the appropriate date. Equally, the returns of the different forms of insurance can be monitored more easily and a far more comprehensive analysis of differing risks be made, making the actuary's life somewhat less hazardous. The reliance on the computer can be seen by the sheer size of data-processing departments some of which employ up to 600 people. Work methods have changed as has the emphasis on the type of work done in the different departments, while the computer has certainly aided the move towards mergers and the concentration within the industry.

Banking concerns have used the computer virtually since its inception, especially the big joint-stock banks. At the time of writing, almost all branches of the 'Big 3' were on-line. The clearing of cheques, cash levels and cash flows, inter-bank commerce as well as the usual personnel functions are performed on computers. Building societies record investment and bill mortgages in the same way that banks issue computerised statements. Theatre and airline seat bookings, indeed the scheduling of the aircraft themselves are now extensively controlled by the use of 'real-time' computer techniques, allowing for greater accuracy at greater speeds. Bets are recorded on computers, laundries check ownership and bills with computers, dairies and butchers use computers. If this seems rather like Charlie Chaplin's 'Modern Times' it most assuredly is not; yet customers have noticed little difference between that fictitious forecast and the present because although the service is supposedly more efficient there are fewer people to complain to when mistakes are made and the staff who are complained to merely blame and then pass on the complaint to the data-processing department.

For the staff themselves there have been changes. The first has been when a stricter compartmentalisation of jobs has occurred, each person now undertaking a far smaller range of responsibilities than previously. Secondly, there have been in some instances, very large redundancies. Thirdly, traditional promotion prospects have changed in that the skills that were needed for promotion some 10 years ago have now become fragmented between several individuals rather than vested in just one. This has hit hardest at those who joined an organisation say 20 years ago with definite ambitions and goals but have found these goals changing and are reaching the age where they do not have time to adapt. There is little inter-change between the data-processing departments and the mainstream of the organisation and this has certainly led to fears and resentments especially in the type of middle-aged employees mentioned above. It might be said that one form of tedium has replaced another overall.

There have been attempts to harness the inherent capabilities of the computer in an imaginative way in this sector of the economy. Computer-dating services is one example, and Ariel, a rival to the Stock Exchange where deals can be made on-line through a computer, bypassing the traditional floor of the exchange, is another. To date at least twenty brokers are subscribers. We have seen computer-based horoscope casting, football, boxing and cricket matches all decided by computer (in fun only); horserace tips, football pools checking (at the cost of many jobs), television's election-night predictions and many others. For the most part there was existing space capacity on existing computers but this type of use does provide programmers and analysts with employment.

The distributive sector uses computers in a big way. On the transport side British Rail uses them for ticket issuing at main line stations, seat reservations, scheduling of traffic, both passenger and freight, and signalling. Although there has been a steady diminution of British Rail's work-force little of this can be laid at the door of their computerised operations, it was more a run-down of lines, although the computer had an analytical role in this analysis. The actual work conditions have changed little except for other technological changes; for example, the switch from steam to diesel or electric locomotion has made life cleaner if less romantic for drivers and firemen but the same pressures remain. In the shunting yards and the stretches of main track the computerised signalling and marshalling systems have cost jobs but here there is a greater degree of responsibility for those working the new systems.

Large road haulage firms and shipping companies use computers for freight recording and scheduling, billing, invoicing and in general a better use of resources. With the growth of containerisation there is now a marked link between sea, road and rail transport and between these and air transport too when the jumbo jets use containers fully in place of the traditional pallets. London Airport already has a computerised cargo terminal. This inter-relation argues for some form of centralised national freight computer which can give a user rapid advice and provide the fastest, most efficient form of distribution, but until each of the users stops actively competing against the other, this will remain a consumers' dream. In shipping there has certainly been a loss of jobs consequent upon computerisation as many of the traditional shipping clerks' functions have been made redundant and those remaining often act as mere information collectors for the installation.

On the other side of the distributive industries, retailing and wholesaling, there have been extensive changes. The growth of the supermarket with centrally controlled stock-holding has forced the small shop out of business. It has of course cut prices to the consumer in most instances and it has also changed job functions quite remarkably. Shop managers have some, but diminished, discretion in ordering, and assistants have been replaced by check-out personnel. The growth in these chains, and their cheapness which makes them attractive to shoppers, could not have been sustained without the computer exercising stock and cost controls.

The wholesale sector is somewhat different although here too, away from the public eye, agencies have sprung up coordinating market supplies and using the computer to coordinate. Wholesaling demands the bulk movement and storage of goods and with the high rates of interest that have prevailed over the last few years, the holding of stocks becomes an expensive business unless their prices appreciate faster than the prevailing interest rates. As wholesale goods are not generally in this 'old master' category, computers have been used to work out the optimum buying, selling and holding times as well as to record stocks, to invoice, etc. The computer may well ultimately hold transactions rather like the Ariel computer and providing that sample testing can be arranged, obviate the need for large bulk carriers or long journeys to a central market, only for the goods to return to their area of origin for retailing.

The final sector is the Government sector. Local and central government and the quasi-independent government agencies use computers to a great extent. They are used for several basic functions such as data collection for statistical series, research, forecasting, service functions such as remuneration and pensions, tax, rate and rent collections, defence, health and education. This formidable and certainly non-exclusive list is matched by the large number of installations and the staffs required to service them. There is, as previously mentioned, a central agency dealing with procurement of machinery and its running but each department has responsibility for its own data-processing work.

Central government departments are heavy users of computers with not only central installations but installations in the various sites, plants and offices around the country. The staff are either recruited as executive or clerical grade staff and then trained or are hired as trained personnel into the administrative or specialist grades. There is, however, as in the other sectors a lack of appreciation of the strengths and weaknesses of data-processing in the senior echelons of the Civil Service, a weakness which the Civil Service is aware of, and is committed to eradicate. Each department will have its own uses for computers. The Treasury will undertake what passes for economic forecasting and predictions of the results of a change in taxation; for example, the Inland Revenue section will use computers to check, demand and record tax payments. The Ministry of Defence has several installations, some central, some attached to various sections of the three armed forces, some in research and others in production sectors. In each department such as Health and Social Security or Trade, there will be several installations, for the recording of data, remunerations, etc. It is, in this complex age, true to say that the modern government department could not function without computers, yet the impact on the Civil Service staff as a whole has been small. The tensions and jealousies have appeared as in the other sectors but the departments and the Civil Service itself are large enough to provide career structures in all areas and thus limit the potential conflicts, which the private sector has not managed to do.

One installation that has worried many of the Civil Service unions is the Civil Service department's manpower data-base – PRISM. Data-bases are one of the trendier computer concepts and mean (in a most generalised way) the pooling of all available information about a subject or organisation. The worry that the unions have is that the employers will not only be able to project manpower requirements (which in itself may be desirable) but that they now have all known facts of employees centralised and recorded. From the inception of computers it was realised that security of information and privacy was both at risk and paramount – unfortunately the measures that are really needed to secure guarantees are not being taken and a central data-bank is vulnerable not only to extra-legal abuse but to future political abuse too. This problem of security and privacy of information will be discussed in more detail in Chapter 4.

Local government is also a large computer user for rate and rent records and for buying, ordering and accounting, etc. It is a sobering thought but as local government powers decrease, so the size of the administrative unit and the number of installations and staff increase. Other public sectors use computers too. The National Health Service has central departments, Regional and Area Health Authority and individual hospital installations, some of which perform service functions, while others have medical or research functions. We are indeed reaching the stage in medical research where the systems analyst is as important as the basic researcher while the doctor now has to have a working knowledge of the computer. Job placement through the Executive and Professional Register is already linked in various cities by a computer system and the Department of the Environment and the Manpower Services Commission intend to follow the Swedish system of extending this to all employment exchanges or as they will be known 'Job Shops', providing a self-service country-wide coverage.

Universities all have computer departments for teaching and research purposes and as in medical research so in disciplines as disparate as sociology and physics, the use of data-processing is becoming essential and in a sense researchers have been forced to become multi-disciplinary. In all of these types of installations there are specialist staff in the data-processing departments but it is assumed in most universities that the individual user will have some knowledge of techniques even though he or she may be say, a botanist!

The government and public sector data-processing requirement is very wide-ranging and varied. The job impacts are there but the sector tends to a stricter job definition system than the private sector and also operates a more rigid grading structure. This, plus advanced consultation with the appropriate unions, has allowed for a relatively smooth operation even to the extent of decentralising from London, for example, to Swansea for driving licences and to Norwich for the National Computer Centre itself. Some of the government sectors have not, however, progressed quite so smoothly. There are certainly problems appertaining to local government and universities both of which have decentralised bargaining for at least the 'top-up stage' of payments for skills and where reorganisation has caused some serious organisational problems.

This has, of necessity, been a sketchy overview of the application of the computer and computerised techniques to British society in general and to employees in particular. It is far from being an exhaustive list of computer functions and was not intended to be so. It has, however, indicated the grip that data-processing has on the economy and some of the problems and dangers it has caused or may cause. Chapters 2 and 3 may have seemed excessively gloomy in that the positive side of computers was not stressed, indeed only grudgingly acknowledged. There is an excellent reason for this.

This book is about computers and unions and how they inter-relate. The sad fact is that when an installation is set up with no problems, all the staff are retained, good retraining schemes are used and if no problems ensue either the unions have been involved at an early stage and pre-empted the trouble or there has been no need for the unions to become embroiled. Rather like all news being bad news, the computer in industrial relation terms spells trouble for trade unions' professional officers, if it is brought to their attention at all. Thus unions have to concentrate on the unfortunate side effects of computerisation; it is similar to trade unions only being in the news when they strike with no great detail being given to the cause or a settlement.

In all the sectors there are trade unions, some weaker than others, some smaller than others, but the overall coverage is wide. It takes in the unskilled, the skilled, clerical, scientific, technical and managerial staff, indeed all employees who either work with computers or are affected by them. Obviously not all these employees are members of unions, the percentage penetration into each sub-sector differing widely but all employees have the opportunity of joining and many of those who do not join are covered by collective agreements and negotiations carried out by the unions. As was pointed out at the start of this book some employees have benefited, others have suffered because of increasing computerisation and the remainder of this book deals with the struggle of unions to come to terms with what is potentially a machine of enormous benefit to their members.

Chapter 4

The public face

There are over 10 million employees who are members of trade unions affiliated to the Trades Union Congress and roughly another 1 million in unions or quasi-unions not so affiliated, but over 15 million employees are affected directly by their negotiations. When the families, that is children in full-time education and elderly dependants, are included the number of people in Britain affected by trade-union agreements is nearer to 36 million or 64 per cent of the total population. This makes it by far the largest, and practically the most significant and powerful, coherent grouping in national life; the wonder is that its influence has never been exploited. If one compares this figure with that of the self-employed, directors or any other group, even the sex groups of men or women, unions dwarf them.

Although the basic reason that union members pay their subscription to a trade-union is for services that are provided centering on the work-place, unions have an impact outside this limited sphere. Even in the earliest unions, the fight for better (and less dangerous) working conditions was centred on the loss of the breadwinner and the impact this would have on the remaining family. Many of the early unions also had as their main function Friendly Society objectives and it is interesting to note that nationally this tradition is maintained because, apart from a short hiatus caused by the 1971 Industrial Relations Act, trade unions register with the Registrar of Friendly Societies. There is thus a tradition in the movement of caring for and taking action on behalf of the families of union members.

Running alongside this are the political and social objectives and functions of trade unions. The Labour Party as we know it today was created out of the need for the trade-union movement to have a political effect and rather than combine the industrial and political functions the Labour Party was formed to be the political spearhead. By and large this arrangement has worked well although there are some who would complain that you would be hard put to realise the close connection between the two. The unions have seats on the National Executive Committee of the Labour Party and a TUC–NEC liaison committee exists and meets regularly. Unions have also had a series of social objectives on which they act as a pressure group. The latest of these has been the campaign to increase the old-age pension, but there have been several others ranging from free education and health services to housing and nuclear disarmament. It should therefore come as no surprise to realise that unions have an interest in what happens to the families of their members and are prepared to take action on their behalf should there by any disquietude.

The computer affects every one of us in Britain, unless some people have managed to 'drop out' to the extent of not paying rates or rent and are self-sufficient in all other respects. It is true, however, that few people realise either the effect or the existence of the computer even when it stares them in the face, as on all bank cheques or credit cards. This should not be wondered at too much as generally the consumer neither thinks nor cares about the process behind a good or bad service, but just accepts the service given, and there are few reasons why a consumer should look behind the facade. This only happens if a process goes wrong or there is an error and it is then that the procedures behind the mistake are brought into the open; the bank statement crediting £150,000 too much, the gas bill for £1,000 or the uncancellable magazine subscription all bring the use of the computer into focus.

There are some areas where the use of the computer is open, indeed its use is the basis for an advertising campaign. The computer-dating services, and there are many of them, actually promote themselves by playing on the belief that the machinery is somehow infallible. Given the range of questions asked on subscribers' forms and the rather strong likelihood that they will not be answered honestly, this belief must be shattered in many cases. It is of course a case of the computer performing adequately, but the results only reflecting the quality of the data submitted. Another case of deliberate advertising is in police work, especially in the USA where it is hoped that the publicity suggesting that computers make crime detection more efficient will deter potential criminals from committing offences. Although we do not know what the crime rate would have been without such techniques neither the rate of offences committed nor the detection rate give much credence to the campaign.

Bills and invoices generally arrive on the public's doorstep having been printed out by a computer although few people recognise this. The installations which produce them may be in-house, especially tax and rate demands and bills from the larger commercial companies or hire-purchase agencies. Equally few people realise that their cheques are cleared or their building society repayments credited on computers. When this does become apparent is when, as mentioned above, mistakes are made. This realisation is driven home because when a complaint is made the employees who normally have to deal with the public have no method of solving the customer's problem without reference to the data-processing department. Such a situation which is out of the employees' control can be most worrying and lead to quite radical job dissatisfaction. On the other hand it can be argued that as fewer mistakes are made the front-line employee's job has become easier.

What is also apparent is the increasing number of complaints about some services and even more worrying the increasing number of complaints about unhelpful staff. It is in this latter area that trade unions become actively involved. This is when the employer takes what the employees and the union consider to be unfair disciplinary action against the employee, which at its most extreme is dismissal. Although some complaints are obviously justified, many should really be levelled at the data-processing department but it is the customer-contact employee who has to bear the brunt of what are often personal attacks and does on occasion retaliate verbally in self-defence.

There are, however, some jobs where the front-line staff have a palpably more pleasant and satisfying job as a result of a computer installation. An example of this is the staff who provide information about flights at airports and book seats for passengers. Where previously there were several reference books to consult and none of these gave any indication of cancelled flights, bad weather or delays of any description there is now a real-time computer system. This saves time, is far more accurate and has cut the number of complaints about staff very drastically and in turn this makes the job far more pleasant, although the commercially necessary though anti-social practice of over-booking flights still rebounds on the innocent employee. Large theatre and hotel booking agencies and coach firms use the same system (though not of over-booking) and have experienced the same staff effects.

Computers, like all new machinery and systems may have teething troubles. It is not advisable, however to allow these to impinge on the service to customers. The Driving Licence Centre in Swansea is a case in point. Where previously the Local County Authority was responsible for the issue and the renewal of drivers' licences, this has now been centralised under the aegis of the Department of the Environment. Unfortunately the system, which in both capital-cost terms and staffing and running costs is roughly twice as expensive as predicted, is about only half as efficient as the old system. There are long delays; lost forms and marginally wrongly entered forms mean that the driver has to start all over again, rather like snakes and ladders. It is this lack of foresight that characterised the initial computer boom in the 1960s and which makes the public sceptical of the computer in general. Dentists have had the same problem since computerised forms had to be submitted to the Estimates Board for payment. Those dentists who bother to check their returns against submissions have found a marked increase in errors made, apart from the fact that the form itself seems to take twice as long to fill in as the old one.

There would seem to be a shift in work done when a computer is introduced into these sort of areas. Although for the centralised body it may be more efficient and time-saving, those who have to provide the information need additional time to do so. There is thus a redistribution of total work time onto the beneficiary of the service himself or herself. Occasionally, however, mistakes occur, sometimes with alarming implications. The public was made aware that the Department of Trade uses a computer when it was announced that due to a program error the Balance of Payments statistics were wrong by a standard £30 million per month. The disconcerting issue here is that although this was reflected in publicly available statistics, how many times has it happened before when the purpose of the exercise was to give advice to a Minister who then took action on that advice. The computer gives the civil servants a very powerful new weapon, especially if one considers that in essence they are professionals and the Minister a dependant amateur.

Some years ago the Government set up the Younger Committee on Privacy. The fact that they felt impelled to do so was a good measure of the disquiet being felt about the privacy and security of information especially with regard to computers. Each list of subscribers to a service or product, each list of defaulters on payments, each list of any description other than random will be of use to someone and the computer stores on disc can then point out such information. The Post Office employees had an argument with the Post Office at one stage over the large quantities of cheap unsolicited 'junk mail' which was increasing their work-load. This plethora of communications was only made possible by computerised listings and mailings. The question is: is such a mailing an intrusion on the individual's privacy?

The trade unions helped the National Council for Civil Liberties to present evidence to the Younger Committee on two grounds. The first was the protection of the individual at large – that is a union member in his or her capacity as a consumer or the family of a union member; the second was in the industrial environment. The industrial question will be dealt with in a subsequent chapter, the consumer aspect, however, must be dealt with now.

When data-banks of names are built up and maintained there are generally far more facts on the form which the client originally filled in than are needed for the service actually provided. It is thus possible to abstract certain groups of people and sell lists of them to other concerns, who can then mail, pester or otherwise intrude on the lives of members of the public who do not want their services. The scale of a data-bank may be of the whole list or just selected parts of the list, for example all married men with two children or all single women under the age of 60, or perhaps all those with good credit ratings. At a Congressional hearing in the USA Robert Westin defined privacy as 'the right of the individual to control the information about himself that he chooses to share with others, how he shares it, when he gives it', etc. This must include personal addresses.

Patently many of the parties involved in data-bank transactions infringe this definition, yet few are extra-legal. When the Fire, Auto and Marine Insurance Company went into liquidation, the liquidator sold the tapes as second-hand computer tapes for £50; someone bought cassettes literally worth millions of pounds for this trifling sum. On the tapes were names, addresses, ages, marital status, dependants, ability to pay premia, type of car, job, health and a host of smaller details, invaluable not only to insurance companies but many other organisations. Not only did hundreds of thousands of motorists lose a considerable amount of money, they also lost a considerable amount of privacy. In the USA such a sale for such an amount could not happen, since these data-banks are sold in liquidations for considerable sums of money. Some organisations have been built up by offering these intrusive services. For example, central credit-rating agencies not only build up a central register of defaulters but one agency actually issues a circular stating that unless the bill is paid the customer will 'lose their total credit-worthiness forever'. Private detective agencies offer, as a service, retrieval of information from data-banks, and on a wider scale it is asserted that there is a link between the Driving Licence Centre installation at Swansea and police installations. This wide dissemination of information, outside the control of the unwitting donor cannot be in the public interest as a whole; the implications and the possible misuses are disturbing in the extreme.

This overt dissemination plus the lack of security surrounding data-banks has not yet reached the public consciousness, although from time to time some TV investigating programme presents a feature on a family being prosecuted for non-payment of bills which they had never incurred. This, however, is treated as an aberration of the system, rather than a product of the system and the more basic question goes unnoticed and unanswered. That there are questions to be answered is not in doubt, but who will do the questioning and who is responsible for answering is uncertain. One argument is that the trade unions themselves should take action in that they should not condone overtly anti-social practices.

This is not a new solution. From the time the dockers refused to load ships in London Docks with arms bound for the Whites during the Russian Revolution there have been social strikes or boycotts. The boycott of Californian grapes from 1968 to 1970 mainly by trade unionists and their families in both the USA and the rest of the world forced the USA grape-growers to recognise the trade unions, indeed this and the potential dispute between the Post Office and the Union of Post Office Workers (UPW) were both socially oriented (see p. 34). Recently the employees at Lucas's submitted a detailed case as to why they should be, and would prefer to be, engaged on socially useful work rather than the military contracts on which they were working. Perhaps an even better example comes from Australia where the New South Wales Builders' Labourers' Federation have imposed forty-two 'Green Bans' including refusing to demolish houses for motorways, refusing to build a car park for the Opera House in the Botanical Gardens and the refusal to demolish buildings of historic interest. At the same time they argue for a rational use of building resources; more flats, hospitals and schools and fewer office blocks, their argument being that workers should demonstrate a sense of social responsibility. This argument could well be extended to the social implications of data-banks. The UPW showed a possible way by concentrating on one of the end products, but surely unless remedial and corrective action is taken on access to, including security of, such information, those running the installations could well demonstrate their sense of social responsibility. British employees have in the past demonstrated that social injustice and inequities would not be tolerated by them and one suspects that as pressures build up on computer use and there is no response from the users to the pressure, that action will be taken.

Not only is this not a new argument as far as trade unions are concerned, it is also a variant on the traditional scientist's dilemma. Although highlighted by the nuclear fission case, it extends far beyond this into most realms of science, biology, chemistry and even mathematics. Should a scientist work on research when the political use of that research may be, in the scientist's opinion, anti-social? The atom and hydrogen bombs had their research drop-outs, some before Hiroshima, some after and continually scientists move away from germ-warfare or gas and chemical experimentation. As the potential of data-collection becomes apparent, and this will only be if examples impinge upon the public, so the data-processing dilemma will grow, and although unions will undoubtedly play their part, it may be that, as with scientists, individual senior analysts or managers will lead the way.

There are other areas where computers impinge on the public, although not always in the full public glare. When Ms or indeed Mr Smith does the weekly shopping the odds are that most of the non-durable goods will be bought in a supermarket and that this will be a branch of a large chain. A major reason for the growth of these chains has been the centralised stock control that can be exercised given a computer. Of course, stock controls can be exercised without such a method but the sheer size of a modern operation would make manual centrally-based control slow and unreliable. Through this control the supermarket chain can minimise its holding of stocks (given a fast distribution of goods) and thus also minimise its overheads and ease its cash flow position. Although chain supermarkets realise that there are regional differences in consumer preferences, the basic goods offered are standardised and the regional preferences are standardised, too. Overall this gives a far smaller range of goods offered to the consumer, who, although able to exercise choice in principle, only has a choice in respect of an already chosen bundle of items. This restriction, a direct result of mass organisation, is only symptomatic of the restrictions placed on durable good choice by mass production and fits neatly into Galbraith's now famous theory that the consumer is no longer sovereign, the manufacturer makes the basic choice; what the computer has done is to extend this to the retail trade.

There is of course little that trade unions can directly do about this phenomenon, though certainly the job of the shop assistant has become far less interesting and indeed has changed to a shelf replenisher and till manipulator.

Overall, the computer should have provided a more efficient service to the public either through improved government services or through improved consumer services. In some sectors this has undoubtedly happened – in others the use of the computer to increase the size of the operation has decreased rather than increased the quality of services available and reinforces tendencies towards feeling isolated in today's world. This is felt both by the employees in the ever-growing departments of corporations and the individual in relation to government. Size can be a great inhibiting factor dwarfing the status of the individual and creating the sort of feeling one gets physically when strolling down the 'Wall Street Canyon'. It is of course not only the employee who feels the impact. The consumer, confronted by shelves of goods and a fast-moving check-out counter instead of the service-oriented shop can be overawed and subdued. Dealings with public utilities, government departments, even local authorities become that much more remote and thus inhibiting. In short as units grow larger, so the point of human reference recedes and the ability of an individual to control his or her life diminishes.

Chapter 5

Changing patterns

No society is static, it is dynamic with the ebbs and flows of tides between fashions, between politics and policies, between rival economic theories and superimposed on all this the impact of ever-changing technologies. A static society would soon die, bereft of innovation, sterile of ideas and bored to death. As the fashions change they involve changes in the means of production and thus changes in employment both within the industry that has become fashionable and the other industries and sectors in the economy from whom skilled and unskilled employees must be seduced. Each country proceeds at its own pace and in its own way, constrained of course by the fact that it has to co-exist in the world, exporting the things it can make, dig out or grow, while almost certainly importing goods of many descriptions from other countries.

Britain, certainly since 1945 has assumed a strange, sometimes rolling or crablike gait towards its unknown goal, so that by 1976 it has become an industrial country without a solid manufacturing industry base and a large consumer of foodstuffs without an agrarian base. To discover exactly why or how this unfortunate state of affairs has emerged could produce enough paper-work, which, if laid end to end would certainly exceed the length of all the computer print-outs made in Britain last year. One thing, however, that most people agree on is that there has been a lack of manufacturing investment relative to that made in rival industrial economies. We then run bang up against a few contradictions.

The first is that if there has been so little investment there must have been a low rate of profit or at least inordinately high corporate taxation, because profits must be reinvested. After all most people don't stuff their mattresses with money as that is a sure recipe for losing it to a combination of burglars and inflation. Yet neither is true. Up to the depression in 1974 the return to capital declared in Britain was as high, if not higher than in most other countries and certainly several other industrial nations tax company profits far more steeply than Britain does. The money must have gone somewhere and herein lies one of the problems. British manufacturing industry distributes more to its shareholders and retains less of its profits for reinvestment than most of its competitors. What then happens to the distributed profits because they too have to go somewhere? The answer, again unfortunately, is that they either get channelled abroad, reinvested in Government securities or invested for supposedly short-term gains like property speculation often by the financial institutions, i.e.

precisely those which are supposed to take the longer view. Add on to this the highly glamourised financial operations of the early 1960s, the resulting asset stripping, and the collapse of the fringe banks and one starts to see some reason for the decline.

The next inconsistency is that unemployment has never been much over 1 million or 5 per cent of the working population in this period although 1976 and 1977 will prove that there is no magical amulet against it happening. Manufacturing industry jobs have been lost at a great rate, a rate not fully reflected in the poor and now falling gross investment figures. Those displaced, along with the school and university leavers, took their places in society in the commercial or service industries, local government, central government, Health Service, education and so on. Yet Government revenue was never quite sufficient adequately to fund the increase of public investment then needed. The Keynesian notion of government expenditure substituting for failing private investment obviously, in hindsight, depends on some continuance of total growth and that is precisely what we have not had in any significant measure for many years.

There has thus been a drift from employment in manufacturing to the government, distribution and service sectors. The drift has been reinforced by the switch from the other traditional industries like mining, textiles and railways to the newer, more capital intensive sectors of petro-chemicals, electronics and motor-car manufacturing. Although the non-manufacturing sectors need to employ very many manual workers the overall tendency has been for the white-collar section to grow at the expense of the manual sector. This in turn has been reinforced by the manufacturing sector itself employing an ever increasing percentage of white-collar staff. There are thus two separate but inter-related trends towards the growth in the number of non-directly producing white-collar employees.

This is not a new phenomenon, nor provided that investment in manufacturing industry had been high enough, it is necessarily a bad one. As far back as 1965 the Labour Government introduced the Selective Employment Tax which was designed to discriminate in favour of productive workers. It had little positive impact and may even have been retrogressive and inflationary. This drift of productive to non-productive employment, has had vast economic implications as we can now all see, but for the purposes of this book it is the implications for trade unions, their actions and their growth, which will be emphasised. Whereas up to certainly the 1950s the manual workers' unions were central to the Trades Union Congress membership, in total percentage terms this is rapidly changing and will probably soon be upset to show a white-collar majority. The TUC, however, in some ways still relates to mechanisms which were applicable before the drift started to accelerate.

Although the impact of the computer is universal, those affected in the greater numbers are in the white-collar section in all four sectors, whether employed on the installations themselves or merely having a direct or indirect contact. Because of this the manual unions have had less interest in the problem and less incentive to take up issues on a national level. This may be one of the major reasons why employers have managed essentially unobstructed when it comes to installations and why there has been little evidence of overt national union interest on the privacy issue. However, now that the balance is starting to tilt it may be that this attitude will change and that the union movement will show interest in and concern at the steady, unchecked, untrammelled advance of computers and computerisation.

The drift to the non-manufacturing, white-collar employment sectors has also changed the attitudes of union members themselves. Away from the shop-floor atmosphere and the working environment the average employee finds that communication with fellow employees is that much easier and that by and large there is a more relaxed atmosphere even if the actual work is as hard and the pressure as great. This in turn gives time for awareness to grow and subjects such as computer involvement in jobs seep into everyday conversation. This pressure, from the bottom upwards, on unions whose members are involved in the white-collar field and the relevant industries will ultimately guarantee that the TUC will have to make representations to government on computers, automation and all the related techniques.

The newer growth industries in Britain are basically heavily capital intensive. Petro-chemicals – an industry which should be stimulated by the North Sea and Celtic Sea oil deposits, is a typical example and uses computers in abundance. Electronics, which includes computer and data-processing equipment manufacturing, is by and large capital intensive as is nuclear power, telecommunications and a variety of manufacturing industries varying from shoes to frozen foods. The commanding heights of the economy, were, when Aneurin Bevan coined the phrase, coal, steel, textiles, railways and shipbuilding, i.e. those industries which were heavily labour intensive and have since shed a considerable number of employees, a considerable amount of output and many companies. The commanding heights are now machine dependent. Interestingly the older, now declining industries were single union industries or had at least one very dominant union. The newer industries have a very fragmented membership across both the manual and white-collar sectors and this makes for more competition and (hopefully) better services to members; even in the trade-union movement fashions, modes and techniques change.

But even the most unexpected sectors are becoming more capital intensive: shipping with supertankers and small crews as well as computerised billing and movements; insurance; banking with a terminal in every branch; and the 'City', with rival forms of data-processed bargains. However, these are the industries where the labour force far from being reduced overall, has been increased even though there have been extensive mergers and closures and computer introduction. As real incomes have risen it was to be expected that the overall savings ratio would rise proportionately (assuming a uniform change over the whole distribution range) and this in turn would provide more business for banks and insurance companies and thus indirectly to the City. As world trade increases so does shipping business, especially as the Suez Canal was closed for so long; so the fact that these industries still have a burgeoning demand for employees despite all the conditions which would superficially lead one to believe the opposite, is not then so surprising.

The rates of growth and decline are not necessarily steady. We have seen the National Coal Board advertise for miners in 1974 and 1975 yet the industry has contracted out of all recognition since 1945. We have also seen substantial reductions in 1975 and 1976 of the number of car industry workers, an industry with a history of expansion. The years 1975 to 1977 will surely see contractions of the labour force in all sectors, although some industries will go against the trend and one suspects that both local and central government will shed less than the other sectors. Each boom and slump has had the same effects.

Within this changing society unions recruit their members. Of a workforce of about 24 million over 10 million are members of TUC-affiliated bodies, about 2 million are ineligible or self-employed and roughly another million are in non-TUC-affiliated bodies. The white-collar sections are the fastest growing in union membership terms and also have far the greatest potential for growth. Later in the book we shall deal with recruitment in the computer field but in this chapter we will deal briefly with the general philosophy.

Unions can be aggressive or passive recruiters. ASTMS has a reputation for being aggressive, partly because of its image and partly because of its use of public advertisements; it is, however, one of the more passive recruiters overall, that is to say, potential members have to approach the union first. While a union's power and influence is broadly measured by the number of its members there is an incentive to recruit as many members as possible. This is not an inalienable rule, for example the National Union of Miners with a declining membership and now no longer one of the larger unions, has influence out of proportion to its membership because of its bargaining position and its use of that position.

Employees join trade unions for a variety of reasons, a few of the main ones being a possible cultural ethos to do so, low wages, job insecurity and bad working conditions. Whatever the reason there will be a reason. Few people will pay a subscription to any organisation, or for that matter any money to any organisation unless it serves some purpose to the individual, even charity contributions tend to make the donor feel better. Some industries, especially those in a state of flux, seem to be rushing to trade unions for some form of representation in ever-increasing numbers, for example the data-processing industry itself and some specific grades of employees are joining unions in increasing numbers.

The junior and middle management grades typically used to be considered to be outside the trade union catchment area in the private sector. This is certainly not true of local and central government where there has been a long history of unionisation right up to very senior levels. Over the past few years, however, there has been a very marked difference in attitude in the private sector as, increasingly, managerial employees join either white-collar unions or form their own non-TUC-affiliated organisations. These latter groupings range from the Steel Industry Managers' Association with bargaining rights to the smaller and more general managerial, engineering and scientific associations with few agreements and little prospect of any growth.

Computerisation has, in many instances provided the spur directly and indirectly for this stampede to the unions. Computers have brought about rationalisation among managerial grades and have aided company mergers and takeovers. In either case there is considerable doubt about future prospects. especially promotion prospects. With this doubt there dawns a recognition of the fact that managers are only employees, capable of being fired, and with it the need for trade-union representation. Often, once a computer is installed, managers are called upon to exercise different and new talents and learn new techniques; many feel that they are too old to do so or lack the faith in themselves to do so, and the consequent uncertainties lead to trade-union membership. The final computer-oriented reason for joining a trade union is more subtle and probably more important.

One major effect of a central computer installation is that the databanks hold all the useful available information. Senior management who have control of the information are the only people in a position to hold an overall view of the concern. As industry becomes more specialised so we get greater divisions of labour and this applies as much to management as to the shop-floor. What tends to happen is that whereas in the past middle management retained their own records and received general circulars containing other peoples' information and could thereby build up their own picture of the concern, information is now rationed. Certainly there was an incredible amount of duplicated data being held and circulated in a variety of places and ways but this did have an advantage to managers. Nowadays a manager receives information which concerns his or her job function and nearly always that alone. He or she will then know about some functions of departments with which they have to deal but will not be in a position to make global assessments of the firm. This puts the manager in exactly the same position as a shop-floor worker, that is, he is expected to do the job and that is all. Imagination can go into decline.

Traditionally in Britain junior and middle managements have held privileged positions and these have manifested themselves in better conditions of service and higher salaries and a more informed position. The last decade has seen a rapid erosion of salary differentials between non-organised middle management and trade unionised non-managerial grades, a constant movement towards the equalisation of status and other conditions of service and finally the computer has removed the information privilege. These factors – the last a considerable status loss to the type of employee in the managerial grades – have convinced many of them that their future is bleak without representation, and that representation must be within a collective bargaining framework. Senior management often opposes the unionisation of its middle and junior counterparts quite immoderately and expresses astonishment at their apparent willingness to abandon the protective umbrella of the internal company hierarchy. What the senior people do not seem to realise is that it is they themselves who closed the umbrella. The whole phenomenon is inevitable once information rationing is introduced and the process will be accelerated far faster when the Planning Agreement system provides more information about the future of the concern to independent trade-union members than middle management grades can possibly hope to get.

The plight of the managers, and their most sensible reaction to it, is echoed by that of other non-managerial employees in all walks of life; that is to say that the computer has changed job prospects and social thinking. The whole range of the movement to capital intensity has also had other repercussions. Equipment even if it works by itself or with a minimum of supervision, cannot function entirely on its own – it needs servicing. There has consequently been an increase in the number of service engineers, an increase which in itself has taken up a considerable amount of the manpower loss caused by automation. It has been said that we are well on the way to becoming a nation of service-engineers, bunny girls and clerks which is not a hopeful proposition. A consequence of this service orientation is that union action becomes more difficult to take. A feature of the life of service personnel is that they work in various locations, often having to spend a considerable amount of time away from home rather like a commercial traveller. This obviously, leads to a lack of contact and a lack of cohesion which mitigates against industrial action should it be necessary. Successful disputes have taken place but the organisation needed for it is quite substantial and has to be sophisticated.

Among the industries changing in the eddies of this society is the data-processing industry itself. It is not unique in being subject to the pressures of a cyclical economy although its collapse in 1971 was more pronounced, and nor is it alone in being in a state of technological change, although the change may be greater in this industry than in most others. Nor is it alone in being affected by the Common Market although again this is the industry in which the Commission has taken a special interest.

The United Kingdom's membership of the Common Market is now, after the Referendum in June 1975, an established though in some quarters a still controversial outcome. The European Commission is charged under the Treaty of Rome with many functions including the harmonisation or 'sameness' of certain industrial practices among other things, and it is also bound by resolutions of the Council of Ministers among which ranks the creation of European Companies. Add to this a rather indefinite yet enforceable article of the Treaty of Government aid to industries or companies which might 'distort competition' and there is a distinct possibility that EEC intervention will take place in many sectors over the next few years. The computer and peripheral manufacturing sectors have been singled out by the Commission for special action partly on the ground of European harmonisation and partly to fight against what they see as the overwhelming threat of the US multi-national International Business Machines.

The actions outlined have very important implications for the major British manufacturers – e.g. International Computer Ltd. The Common Market recommendations are based on the premise that the growth areas in the immediate future will be in peripherals, mini-computers and software mainly at the expense of the large installation. There is of course, no way of verifying this premise but the conclusions drawn do fit in alarmingly well to the preconceived European notion that the future of a European industry will be to complement IBM products rather than outright competition. It was the rejection of this principle some 5 years ago that prevented ICL from joining the European consortium of German, French and Dutch manufacturers known as Unidata. This consortium has now run up against considerable difficulties which has, in itself raised doubts as to the viability of a European-based industry on existing concepts.

The EEC document contains one passage that needs looking at somewhat more closely – 'that is why it [the Commission] considers that national governments should only accord further aids in these fields [main manufacturers of central processes] to promote promising associations between European producers'. If this is implemented it means in practice that the British Government could not continue to provide financial assistance to ICL unless it was to promote a link with manufacturers whose marketing and production strategy was totally different. This can only be a recipe for unemployment in this industry in Britain. Does it also apply to aids given through preferential Government ordering? If so the position of ICL and its employees will be even worse. There have been signs that ICL are preparing to adopt the EEC strategy to the grave disquiet of the unions involved.

The whole idea behind the concept is quite acceptable if it is believed that Common Market (as opposed to European) based industries are practicable or desirable. There are plans to develop a special Common Market real-time programming language; plans to encourage portability in peripherals, terminals and compilers; proposals for a potpourri of studies and harmonisations including confidentiality and programming techniques, and the development of a European soft-ware package. While all of these are essential prerequisites for a challenger to IBM to get off the ground, if ICL are to be forced into an unsuitable merger using a system which cuts off Government aid then the British industry will be destroyed. The problem then is that even if after perhaps 10 years when Britain starts to produce again as part of a European industry it will have lost firstly its guaranteed home market and secondly will be unlikely to recoup this loss in its entirety as a joint manufacturer.

This is, naturally, speculation although based on persuasive evidence. The future of British industry and commerce, the employees who work in it and the unions who represent them must be speculative too. With traditional industries declining, but far later than our competitors and our entry into the new, high value-added industries later still, the future is at best, uncertain. The computer came to Britain early but in terms of corporate usage as opposed to corporate access we now lag behind our competitors in yet another sphere. As this argument develops we shall look at the benefits and costs of computerisation and the problems thrown up. What must be clear is that if we intend to compete internationally as an exporter of manufactured goods then the most modern techniques used in the most advanced industries must be the objective. This strategy involves a heavy dependence on computers and if it is successful will almost certainly stimulate manpower changes between economic sectors that make the changes since 1945 trifling and these changes will themselves throw heavy strains on the matrix of society.

Chapter 6

Collective bargaining

The sharp cutting edge of a trade-union organisation is directed towards negotiations with employers and these can fairly be described as the main reason for which the bulk of trade-union members joined in the first instance. Negotiating, or more accurately, collective bargaining, rarely gets publicised in any of the media unless there is a possibility of a breakdown, or indeed there has been a breakdown, in which case the coverage changes to that of an industrial dispute and impending disaster. In an earlier chapter it was pointed out that for the majority of the public, computers only exist when a mistake is made thus drawing the attention of the recipient, or in gross cases the media; in other words there is only recognition of disaster. As trade unions basically only get publicity when a negotiation breaks down, rather than when the overwhelming majority of them settle peaceably, there is a close affinity between computers and unions, that of being one of the media's favourite *bêtes noire*.

Because few people in Britain know anything about collective bargaining, it is often publicly assumed that it is an anarchic process with a preponderance of table-thumping, threats of blackmail, ransom and brute illogicality. Generally speaking nothing could be further from the truth. Negotiations are conducted strictly within a rigid framework known as the Procedure Agreement, a document which delineates the bargaining group or groups in question, the employer (important in a conglomerate situation), the union or unions, what items are to be the subject of collective bargaining and the stages through which bargaining will be taken. A procedure agreement may be many pages long with additional appendices and sometimes elevate negotiations to an industrial ritual of Confuscian reverence and Japanese formality. Such an agreement also lays down the form of negotiation – whether it is to be domestic with a secondary national phase, merely domestic or perhaps totally national, or indeed whether it is to be conducted with a federation of employers.

In practice the procedure agreement dictates not only the form of negotiations but often the outcome. For example, an agreement whose last stage is arbitration will, three times out of four, end up at arbitration, but a procedure which includes only a failure to agree will settle before this – nine times out of ten. A national-level negotiation in a multi-plant or office enterprise may leave scope for local settlements or conversely even local conditions of service may be settled at a national level. An agreement will typically have three or four stages starting with local lay representatives meeting local personnel management, the representatives presenting a claim, negotiation then going on to local professional union officials and up to national officials, while at the same time the management side match seniority with seniority. If at the end of the stages there is a settlement, a collective agreement is drawn up which details all of the decisions. If at the end there is still a difference between the sides, a 'failure to agree' is registered and either an industrial dispute or arbitration settles the matter. Generally neither the collective agreement nor the procedure agreement is legally binding, they are binding in honour only, but such agreements are rarely broken.

Data processing departments are what are known as 'high profile' in industrial relations terms, that is to say that disruption of their normal functions deeply and speedily affects management of departments outside data processing. It is therefore an area which in industrial terms is sensitive. Some jobs, for example in research departments, design offices or procurement are important but their effect on the enterprise that employs them is long rather than short term and disruption of their functions takes a long time to have effects. In industrial disputes this difference is vital, a short sharp dispute is far preferable to one which may drag on for months, preferable in all senses.

It is rapidly becoming clear that negotiations are as much a collective noun as is the word computer in that there are very different types in both style and content. Different subjects for negotiation require different forms of negotiation. In addition there can be a variety of ways by which the subject can be negotiated. For example remuneration agreements can be achieved either by dealing with each topic separately – salaries, holiday entitlements, pensions and so on – or by handling all topics at the same time. There are tactical advantages for both sides in both methods, and while the latter is more common outside engineering it does involve multiple 'trade-offs'. The type of union is also important, although not so much in data-processing. Unions can be specific to a trade, e.g. electricians and the Electrical, Electronic, Telecommunications and Plumbing Union (EETPU), or based on sector, for example NALGO, or can be based on ill-defined status (generally non-TUC-affiliated unions), and finally can be general in that they cover many industries and grades, e.g. TGWU and ASTMS. Obviously the type of negotiation will depend on the experiences of the negotiators and the comparators which are used and in these respects the general union often has an advantage.

In passing, it is worth noting that collective bargaining is not always all about the remuneration package; other matters are negotiated about too. Redundancy is one, either before the event by pre-empting and negotiating no-involuntary redundancy schemes, plus voluntary early retirement schemes or, at the time of the redundancies by trying first to minimise them and secondly get the maximum possible compensation for those who have to go. Disciplinary matters, often taken through a separate grievance procedure are also engaged with. It is in these cases that the essential nature of collectivity in approach is fully revealed; the whole weight of a trade union can be placed behind an individual, who without this support would be totally at the mercy of the employer. These cases apply as much to computer staffs as to any other staffs, and one could in fact unfortunately make a case for the proposition that they applied more because of the jungle-type industrial relations which exist within parts of the industry itself and the rather unstable behaviour of some companies.

In Britain, industry, commerce and the public sector infrastructure are now so highly geared to each other that not only do disputes in one of the sectors have an effect on the others but wage or salary settlements also have a marked effect. Meanwhile the private sector has itself become far more integrated, especially vertically, so that any one action can have most unfortunate repercussions on others, the car industry being a case in point when a small dispute in a component supplier company can affect the livelihood of employees divorced from the dispute and the output of final manufactures. This is increasingly creating more high profile situations which in the sense of effectiveness of trade unions is to their advantage, but in a public relations sense often works in the opposite direction; it is not that strikes are that much more ruthless, it is the structure of the economy which leads to this conclusion after the attendant publicity.

Computer staff grievances, as we have noted, are distinctly high profile issues. As enterprises have adapted to the computer and arranged their information and internal coordination systems to meet its requirements, so they have become more dependent. Fall-back positions are often impossible. For example, how can a large company arrange to pay all its bills, salaries, etc., if all the records are on disc and the clerical type of staff is no longer employed? It is therefore surprising that so few disputes have taken place given the bargaining weapon available. There are four reasons which can be advanced. The first is that employers realise that the weapon exists and always settle to keep the peace although a cursory look at salary increases suggests that this may not be so. A second reason is that no union likes to call out people who are third-party to the dispute in question and the practice of sympathy strikes has diminished as economic integration has advanced. The third reason is the insecurity of data-processing staffs and a fear for their jobs should management retaliate, and finally the lowish penetration of trade unions into the entire area.

But, in the first computer service engineers' strike in the UK in 1964, sympathetic action arrested shops, banks, newspapers, motor plants, Ministry of Labour statistics, and municipal rate collection.

Data-processing staffs not only work in an industry but also work in various industries. This apparent contradiction is because of the diffusion of computer installations and the fact that some of these are in what may be loosely described as the computer industry. The 'in-house' installation obviously refers itself back to the industry in which it is used, whether this is an insurance company, a manufacturing company or a government department. In these instances, and this applies to over 50 per cent of all data-processing staffs, the employer is the industry in which they work and the staff becomes just another group of employees with a skill to sell which is then applied to the function of the employing enterprise. In this way data-processing staffs correspond closely to secretarial staff or professional staff like accountants or solicitors. The computer industry, however, is a combination of computer manufacturers, the bureaux, the agencies, the soft-ware houses and sundry consultancies.

Secretarial skills, like professional skills, are highly portable. A secretary, accountant or doctor is perfectly capable of doing his or her job in different environments, both sectoral and geographical and given the normal constraints of unfamiliarity with equipment, is mobile to an unusually high degree. Basically this same fact applies to computer staff although the equipment side does play a larger role than in the other jobs, as we shall see later. This has an important implication. It means that data-processing staffs are mobile between the industries in which they work and the computer industry itself, and thus one could assume that over time, at least by regional sectors, salaries and conditions of service would tend to equalise. This has not, however, happened and it threatens to become an explosive issue with ramifications far beyond those staff most intimately concerned.

There is an important dichotomy between the manner in which basic salaries are fixed in the industry and in the in-house installation. Salaries in the industry are based on the market knowing that given expertise on certain ranges of equipment staff is totally mobile. As with secretarial staff, however, this does not imply a single wage for each job description or job title, even if such descriptions or titles were in one-to-one correspondence. There are regional and city rates, for example, staff working in central London get a larger premium over those working in other large cities and this may be applied using either an overt London Weighting additional to basic salary, or by just offering a higher basic rate.

The in-house installation, however, not only takes account of the job market prices for the industry, but it also has to take into account its own internal differentials. Within a large head office organisation there is a recognisably stratified pyramid of jobs, each of which carries a differential over the one below it in the pyramid. If, as may happen, a data-processing department is grafted on to this structure the management can either attempt to integrate the new staff into its general grading structure using whichever form of job evaluation its consultancy recommends, or it can place the department to one side. Whichever method it adopts will create problems unless there is a consensus view by staffs and unions that the salaries paid to the staff in the new department are equitable when compared with the rest of the head-office staff. This is unfortunately unlikely to be the case.

To start with, the lack of knowledge of the jobs of computer staff prevents any proper appreciation of their functions or the difficulties inherent in the work, a gap encouraged by the use of the jargon barrier. Secondly, the career staff in the enterprise are generally non-mobile in the extreme, often not even intra-industry and have traded off promotion and security against income and as a result data-processing staff generally are remunerated at a higher rate. In any event it is unlikely that a consensus view will emerge because of the differences in the relationship of the different types of staff to the employing organisation itself. One only has to look at the problems that the escalating rates in secretarial salaries gave in the early 1970s to see the latent problems, latent because data-processing staffs are generally far higher-profile and in company structure terms compete with more senior and thus more entrenched staff. With secretaries, many large organisations found that they had no alternative to using exploited agency staff on a temporary basis because they were unable to recruit typists, etc., at the salaries that their company structures dictated. To offer competitive salaries would have meant a general increase for all staff or risk breaking the structures and few employers wished to do this. Finally this stimulated the now well-documented disputes, in both the private and public sectors against 'temps' which involved strikes and blacking of their work.

Because a large concern has the same problems but in a more acute area, this pull between internal differentials and the industry job market will create ever-escalating problems. A trade union which has members in both the data-processing department and other staff departments is in a somewhat happier position. If there are separate negotiations, one for staff and one for computer staff, it is possible to narrow or widen differentials in one year and then close or open them the following year; there is, in other words, always a bargaining position if not actual leap-frogging. Strangely this method may well be the only way of maintaining industrial harmony as it shows benefits to both protagonists. The alternative is the build-up of agency staff (now starting) on the one hand or a lack of recruitment on the other. There is, in the larger companies, a sharp division of opinion between managements as to the best method to use. In some the bargaining is for all staff, at the same time, regardless of department, allowing internal differentials to stand and keeping the grading system sacrosanct and if this results in a shortfall of computer staffs, using an agency. On the other side of the coin other companies negotiate for computer staff totally separately and this is especially true where the union representing these staff is different to that representing the bulk of employees, as in the Civil Service or occasionally in engineering.

The problem does not often arise where smaller installations in smaller companies are concerned. This is because for a problem to exist there must be overt publicised salary scales and a grading system and many smaller enterprises do not operate on this basis but rather on an *ad hoc* basis.

However, life is not as simple as this. The remuneration package complicates matters as there is often no direct comparability between advertised salaries; the non-salary element in the remuneration package may be as much as 60 per cent of the basic salary itself. This becomes important because by and large the 'fringe benefits' offered by large employers tend to be worth far more than those offered by the computer industry to its staff. One reason is because of the greater union penetration in the large company sector where the white-collar unions have concentrated on remuneration packages for many years, stimulated by successive Government wage restraints which have placed a ceiling on salary increases. Apart from the greater, though by no means absolute, job security which is basically unquantifiable, there are pension schemes, longer holidays, better shift and overtime premia, company cars (still partially untaxed despite the April 1976 Budget), housing aids (such as typical 3 per cent mortgages in the finance sector), subsidised food and specific arrangements like very cheap or free travel, with discounts on products such as cars and clothes. To strike a true comparability between remuneration within the computer industry itself and that paid to staff working in industry or commerce in general, requires knowledge of the amounts needed to fund all these elements on behalf of any one grade of employee. This can be difficult although some comparisons are easier than others. A good pension scheme costs around 18 per cent of payroll, but Civil Service employees effectively have far larger sums placed at their disposal as their scheme is not funded, yet pension schemes within industry (apart from some manufacturers) are on a par with those in the advertising industry, awful or non-existent. Obviously a very young employee will not worry about such a benefit to any great degree, but those somewhat older certainly will.

Yet another problem is comparability of jobs and the tyranny of the job title. In data-processing this is complicated by the vastly different hard-ware and soft-ware used, and thus the different systems in operation which lead to different job functions, although the job title is the same. The job title 'programmer' hides a multitude of different functions sometimes depending on the system in use and sometimes on a function of the internal staffing. Differing systems may be harder or easier to operate, different languages more difficult to learn. There may be only one manager to twenty programmers or one analyst to fifty programs, thus giving the programmers a lot of responsibility and discretion, while in other departments there are nearly as many analysts as programmers. Education complicates matters too. In the early days of computers, the halcyon 1960s, there was an abundance of machines, but a lack of trained personnel. Although there has been a great volume of treatises on the subject there is still a wide disparity in computer education terms and the newish adage that one man's programmer is another man's analyst holds very true. After succumbing to a job description in advertisements the person who takes it is obviously reluctant to take a job of lesser status (or worse description) at a later date: thus we perpetuate a system whereby people, who for no fault of their own are appointed to positions whose title is grand but whose function is ordinary, are forced to trade upwards in job titles. Job evaluation can be of help in these instances, especially if conducted within the data-processing department itself. Its assistance, however, is somewhat limited due to the limitations in job evaluation itself. Job evaluation attempts to rank jobs of totally different skill-levels, responsibility levels, physical endurance levels and so on, yet there are many different forms of evaluation and to be able to read across from one job-evaluated post to another one needs to know what points of weightings or judgements were made in both. Job descriptions can be of more use but again there must be some standardisation of factors and some objectivity for the comparisons to be made without undue hesitation.

These problems have existed in many sectors of employment for a considerable time, indeed the tyranny of the job title is an apt phrase, for people have often been rewarded more in title and status than they were in money. The computer industry is new, it is advanced technology, it is potentially of enormous value, yet this sophisticated, modern, thrusting industry has not learnt from the other's mistakes. Albeit, with higgledy-piggledy growth, troubles were being stored for future generations of users and employees, the only saving grace being where a trade union interposed itself in the bargaining process and sought to bring some order out of chaos.

The growth of the employment or placement agency for data-processing staffs is a portent for the problems in store for the industry. Agencies tend to grow in employment areas where skills are portable: clinical, secretarial, nursing, medicine and draughting and the theatre, and wherever they grow, staff dissatisfaction is not far behind. An agency-temporary employee or fixed-term contract employee generally gets paid a premium over and above the normal rate for similar workers in the same enterprise, the premium compensating for lack of job security and absence of fringe benefits continuity. This higher basic salary is a stimulus to discontent; other employees do not see behind the salary and observe the lack of pension provision, often holiday pay, and other items making up the remuneration package, which the temporary worker does not get. It may well be that the temporary employee is extremely badly off in comparison with his or her colleagues although the cost to the employer is probably the same with the difference being the commission paid to the agency. In some instances of course, mainly those where the package normally offered by the employer is very low on everything but salary, the temporary employee is financially better off and the employer has to pay a total premium after taking the agency commission into account.

Agencies are a constant feature of the data-processing scene. The *Computer Users' Yearbook 1975* lists 108 firms offering recruitment services – some of them deal in full-time placements alone – an increase of twenty-three over the last 12 months and this is in addition to the Professional and Executive Register run by the Government and the ordinary employment services. Alongside this has been the growth in training facilities and establishments which will be dealt with in the next chapter. There are reasons, other than salary, which make employers and trade unions hostile to private employment agencies. The first is that although some are reputable, with trained interviewers, many are the 'two men and a dog operating from a broom cupboard' type of venture, whose interviewing of clients ranges from weak to not at all, whose placements are made primarily to make themselves a profit and when made are so misplaced that they cause annoyance to the colleagues with whom the clients work. A second reason is that agency staff tend not to be trade-union members and some employers have even attempted to staff in data-processing, whole departments, in this way to try and avoid trade-union recognition problems. Finally there is a growing documentation of staff agencies providing blackleg labour during an industrial dispute, as happened recently in the University Computer Staffs dispute. At least one union has attempted to negotiate an agreement with an agency whereby all their placements automatically become members of the union, but the proposal fell. It fell because it could have lead to appalling inter-union problems where placements were made into departments where another union had the negotiating rights. Finally, the Trades Union Congress itself campaigns for the abolition of fee-charging employment agencies and bases this on the International Labour Organisation (United Nations) Convention 96 which states *inter alia* 'Fee charging employment agencies conducted with a view to profit . . . shall be abolished within a limited period of time determined by the competent authority. Such agencies shall not be abolished until a public employment service is established.'

Trade union penetration into data-processing is still very patchy. In the areas of local government, the Civil Service, universities, public corporations and large companies in industrial manufacturing and commercial, there is generally a high degree of union membership. Being a new area, and with data-processing departments added on to existing structures, there have been and will no doubt continue to be arguments as to which unions should represent the staff, although as yet none of these have expanded into dispute situations. There are no problems where there are either agreed demarcation lines as in the Civil Service, or where only one union is recognised in an entire industry or enterprise. The National and Local Government Officers Association is the only body representing white-collar workers in local government and thus all unionised staffs are in this union; ASTMS is the only union recognised by the Prudential Assurance Company and in exactly the same way all unionised computer staffs at the Prudential join ASTMS. However, this arrangement is, in the private sector, the exception rather than the rule, most enterprises being multi-union even in the white-collar sector. There are, in the private sector alone three unions for clerical staffs and another three or four who will accept them into membership and basically seven unions which could claim to represent a few data-processing staff. In any one engineering company it is likely that clerical staff will be represented by one union, supervisors and management by another, drawing office staffs by another and technical staffs by perhaps another. In chemicals, oil and food ASTMS represents across the board but in some manufacturing companies a new department is, in the American vernacular, 'up for grabs' (for example ICI and Fords) and, as a result, computer staffs are courted widely and ardently by a range of suitors.

In the private sector this has meant that unions with what is perceived to be the best track record have gained the majority of members, and ASTMS has a very clear lead across field. It is not of course a race, neither is it any form of sport – employees join a union because among other reasons they feel that they are underpaid, undervalued or insecure in their jobs. Although situated in a new technological sector, data-processing people are certainly joining trade unions especially where there is an existing union ethos. The public sector, especially local and central government, has little in the way of inter-union problems and has a very high union penetration.

In data processing itself the size of the total unit tends to mitigate against trade-union organisation. Most of the bureaux and other agencies are small in total size, generally employing not more than 100 people and often far less. The smaller the unit, the more the personal touch is used to resolve differences and disputes and although this does not often reflect any greater justice or equity it does remove one potent force fuelling unionisation, that of remoteness. In addition the type of staff linked with these small enterprises tend to be risk-takers with the speculative nature of the organisations being reflected in their personnel and again in this instance union membership would be more unlikely. This is, of course not to say that trade unions have no place in this sector or that there is no penetration at all. Certainly some of the larger bureaux are organised and one would expect that with the current uncertainties in the industry and the new recognition procedures in the Employment Protection Act considerably more will follow.

How then, have computer people fared in the chase for adequate standards of living and continuity of employment ('in the chase' because inflation has forced all employees into a drive to maintain the purchasing power of their salaries)? The problem is as follows.

Salaries or earnings are always announced or advertised before the deduction of income tax or national insurance contributions, both of which are income related, while the Retail Price Index, the Government measure of the cost-of-living, is not adjusted for such taxation. This leads to two different considerations. In money terms people are obviously interested in their take-home pay, this being the amount which they have to spend on goods and services each month. Thus for example a married man with two children earning £3,000 per year, has take-home pay of actually £2,243, and obviously there is a shortfall of £757 purchasing power. Let us assume that this man gets a £6 a week increase: after deductions, etc., he gets an actual increase of only £3.60 per week. If the annual inflation rate is above this 8.3 per cent increase the man will be even worse off. His nominal increase was 10.4 per cent with the difference between the two figures resulting from the manner in which British income tax is levied, which is to have initial deductions but a standard rate up to quite large income levels and this distorts the traditional pattern. This has been responsible for the poverty-trap for low income groups and also affects the higher-paid sharply because the marginal rates of tax are that much higher.

It is interesting, if somewhat perverse, to realise that it was the advent of the Heath Government's wage restraint policies Phases I, II and III followed by the Social Contract and the £6 limit which concentrated employees' minds on this phenomenon. It is of course a logical approach and one which was long overdue, although the increasing rate of inflation has exacerbated the problem and led to a position where Press and Government were telling people that they were better off at the same time that they realised themselves that they were worse off. In turn individuals then thought that although they were worse off, other people must have been getting very large increases and they then increased their claims. The policy of deliberately misleading people into believing that union pressure was increasing real disposable income in order to justify a squeeze on earnings was thus quite counter-productive.

Although it would be futile to quote salaries and percentage differentials in a book of this nature because by the time it is read both absolute and percentage amounts will have changed, a quick look at some data will not come amiss. Computer staff salaries, for some reason, seem to attract an inordinate number of surveys which because of the problems of job titling and the drift between basic salary and earnings, are not especially illuminating. They do, however, give some indication of progress even if their use as bargaining tools is limited. The *Computer Users' Yearbook 1975* used fourteen job titles in approximately 1,000 data processing departments covering just over 16,000 staff not including secretaries, data-preparation people, etc. In the period taken the Retail Price Index rose 25 per cent and the index of average earnings rose 28.3 per cent while the median salaries of computer staff rose more slowly. For example, the median salary of data processing managers rose approximately by 17 per cent and that of programmers by 20 per cent. This particular survey shows a marked falling behind of computer staffs in basic salary including overtime and shift premia on some job titles. This may reflect a better than average position at the start of the 12-month period but is, in any event, certainly distorted by the lack of free collective bargaining up to September 1974 and the fact that pre-settlements may have taken place on a catch-up basis after May 1975.

Other surveys show far greater increases, while yet others disagree with the actual gross money levels of salaries paid. Certainly, later salary surveys show a marked catch-up later in 1975 which may well reflect settlement dates. The other point is that within each figure there is a very large range. For example, chief systems analysts' salaries range from £2,500 to £6,500 in departments with up to twenty-five employees, reflecting not only the size of the department but also the difficulty in defining the job. A further difficulty is that the total remuneration package is not taken into account and this, as we have said, can add a substantial amount on to personal disposable income. It is true to say, however, that unorganised computer staffs have not fared well over the last eighteen months, either in relation to other employees in an enterprise. or earnings as a whole; organised ones have at least roughly kept up with the retail price index, in general settlements.

In the next chapter we shall look more closely at bargaining for computer people and at some of the problems that have arisen in the industry.

Chapter 7

Unions meet the computer

There was a song in *Cabaret* entitled 'Money, Money, Money, Money – makes the world go around' which is played as a caricature of a Jew grasping for money in Germany under the Fascists, yet for most people who are not absurd stereotypes money is an important, if not the most important, commodity in life in Britain. Although it is possible to envisage alternative forms of society where this is not the case, so far these are only conceptual. All industrialised societies, whether entrepreneurial, mixed economy or collectivist are firmly based on the principle of consumerism. People are cajoled, intimidated, courted and humoured into buying goods which are surplus to the requirements of ordinary living; advertising and premature obsolescence play their part in stimulating production of these goods and thus work is provided for people to earn the money to buy the goods. Furthermore, the ethos is that the more people buy the higher the standing they get in the eyes of their peers. There is little or nothing material one can personally secure without money and so on, whether we believe that intrinsically this is immoral as some eminent clerics have asserted, the fact is most people in Britain work purely and simply for cash.

People do not work, by and large, because they like the jobs that they do; so many are unpleasant, boring or dangerous, while most others do not allow for any expansion of the individual. Conventional economists take the view that work is a disutility for which the compensation is earnings and at the margin people will prefer leisure to work unless more wages are paid. Although this is a sweeping generalisation because most employees do not have their hours of work within their control, it has been tested among those who do (professional people) and substantially verified. Computer people, some of whom have to work shifts or substantial overtime (both rare occurrences among white-collar workers) are, however, put into a position where they can make some form of trade-off between work and leisure. This is publicly asserted in the willingness to work shifts at various shift payments and to some extent the turnover of staff is not only towards the higher salary job, but to the job requiring either fewer shifts or larger shift premia. Although, as we shall demonstrate yet again, trade unions are not exclusively concerned with money, the demands the membership most frequently make identify salaries as their priority and computer staffs, who are subject to the same pressures as everyone else, are no exception.

Who are computer people? Even when looking at those who work in the hard-ware and soft-ware manufacturing industries does this include the secretarial and clerical staff, the building maintenance staff, drivers and so on? The industry certainly cannot function properly without them yet their skills and experience often have little if anything to do with computers. In a large installation one must include the data-preparation clerks, the porters and the clerks whose function it is to fill in the standard forms before 'punching up'. The Department of Employment has a singular omission in its statistical series in that it does not break down employment in a sub-industrial sector into white-collar skilled or unskilled employments, let alone attempt to define data-processing staffs across industry and commerce. From a trade union standpoint in the real world this point is important in union recognition claims although one can argue that all employees whose jobs are directly dependent upon computers are 'computer people' wherever their expertise lies. For those whose life is dedicated to clarifying various jobs-contents it would be possible to define computer ancillaries and computer employees on a similar basis to the definitions used in medicine which overtly create the distinction between doctors of varying specialities, para-medical staff (radiographers, nurses, etc.), and ancillary staffs.

Within an installation of any reasonable size, that is fifty employees or more, there will be a pyramidal hierarchy starting with porters and reaching a climax with the manager and the salaries paid will reflect the position in the pyramid. There is in other words an intra-location salary differential system which may or may not reflect the differential systems used in the organisation as a whole. In the previous chapter we mentioned the two methods of approaching a data-processing department, that is either by treating it as merely another section in a total regrading, or isolating it with separate salary scales. We shall now look at the implications of these in slightly greater detail.

When data-processing departments were first opened in the 1960s there was general chaos and confusion as to how people should be paid, their levels of pay, and indeed about the total level of staffing. Data-processing managers new to the job were given a relatively free hand by senior management primarily because they were the only people in the organisation with expertise enough to recommend anything to do with the installation. Unfortunately the erratic training facilities then prevailing were combined with the data-processing managers' lack of personnel training resulting in very high staff turnover and an opportunity system of salary settlements in a decade of rapid growth. Such a series of relationships inevitably had to end in economic confusion both from the point of view of senior management whose expectations were not being fulfilled, and the staff who were getting dissatisfied with the lack of career prospects and the uncertainties. This indeed was the era of 'puzzle' advertisements on London Transport which consisted of five diagrammatic arithmetical posers four of which were give-aways and the fifth more difficult, bearing the legend 'if you can solve 4 of these you can have a job in computing' and then gave the name and address of a programmer's course. Many potential trainees were soon bitterly disillusioned by disorganised training and the absence of a career structure. When the economic squeeze came in 1971/72 the computer function was ripe for attack and attacked it was. Sales fell, departments were slashed, budgets cut, cost-effective techniques used and, suddenly, data-processing departments came under both management and union scrutiny. If, in the initial phases, computer staff salaries were high when compared with employees using similar skills, they swiftly fell behind. The myth – and myth it is – of the computer-persons' high salary scales remains, however.

At best data-processing staffs are being remunerated on a par with other staffs and then only because a comprehensive job evaluation has compared all staff within the organisation. In the Civil Service and local government this has long since been done and all staffs are negotiated for at the same time on a national basis. Each job title in the computer department corresponds to a grade in the basic structure and it is thus possible to compare those inside the department to those outside. For example, in the Civil Service a chief programmer, a senior systems designer and an operations manager are in the 'principal grades' and also in these grades are chief work study officers, electrical safety engineers, and deputy superintending plant health inspectors. Although this sounds fine in practice there is a large range of salaries in the 'principal' grade and the trick in both the Civil Service and local government is to get the appropriate department or local authority to move either an individual or a range of employees on to a higher salary range in the grade. It is possible in local government in fact to move up an entire grade or perhaps grades. The Civil Service and local authority trade unions are sophisticated in these techniques.

A variant on this theme is where there has been an overall job evaluation but the grading structure for data-processing staff is distinct and separate. Examples of this method are the Prudential and Norwich Union Assurance companies. Negotiations are on behalf of all staffs and a general increase applied to all departments. This method, as with the Civil Service and local government methods, depends on the salary ratios applicable to the organisation being the same as, or ahead of, those in the industry itself. The difference between the two methods is that at the Prudential, etc., it is difficult accurately to read across job grades other than by comparing salary ranges and certainly almost impossible to do so in an inter-company environment, unless precisely the same job-evaluation techniques have been used.

The final method is like that used at the Midland Bank. In this case there is not only a separate grading structure but also a separate set of negotiations. The salary rates are fixed with regard to the external market rather than the internal structure, although for example data-processing managers would typically be loosely linked to managers within the main system.

If one were to compare salaries (not earnings) across jobs by taking equivalent salary ranges, computer personnel do not compare favourably. For example a data-processing manager receives at present roughly 20 per cent less than a sales manager given an equivalent number of employees for whom they are responsible. To put this in its proper perspective let us compare some of the results in the *Computer Users' Yearbook 1975* salary survey taken in May 1975 with the Government's *New Earnings Survey* taken in April 1975.

The average male non-manual yearly earnings were £3,556 per annum of which only £202 were attributable to overtime or shift premia and payment by results. Fourteen per cent of senior analysts earned less, 54 per cent of analysts earned less, 96 per cent of programmers earned less and 99 per cent of operators earned less. Given these results, even if one were to allow for the computer salaries being on the low side, it is impossible to conclude that computer people are currently well paid. Even taking another and later survey a programmer would have to be over 30 years old and in the top quarter of remuneration to be ahead of national average earnings. The internal ASTMS data does not quite bear this out, as the available statistics show data-processing salaries to be between 15 per cent and 20 per cent higher. Almost all ASTMS data-processing members are in large organisations and it may be that either the unionised sector is paying far higher rates or that the large company tends to pay higher rates or that the samples for the surveys mentioned above were not representative.

The remuneration package, however, makes most of the above data unreliable. There is probably a greater differential between the non-salary elements of the package than that between salaries exclusively. The trade-union movement, especially in the white-collar sector, has taken the initiative in negotiating the elements in the package. If, for example, we take two identically qualified programmers who are both buying houses of identical price, the one in the industry or for that matter in most enterprises, will pay interest on the mortgage of, at present 12¼ per cent, the other working for a financial house or bank or insurance company will pay between 2½ per cent and 5 per cent. While not reflected in the salary level this nevertheless represents a large addition to yearly disposable income, by releasing income which would, for most employees, be tied up in accommodation, to be spent how the person chooses over and above that available to the programmer without this 'fringe benefit'. The same applies to those who get discounted goods – cars (or indeed company cars or car allowances), equipment, food, clothes and even very cheap or free fares on airlines and railways for employees and their families. Some of these benefits may have been made taxable to some extent by the April 1976 Budget, although the Finance Bill has, at the time of writing, yet to be enacted. The proposals, however, do result in increased taxation of some fringe benefits, notably company cars used privately, loans for those earning above £5,000 per annum, mortgages over £25,000 in value and transport and other benefits. When subsidised food and recreation facilities, superannuation schemes, sickness, life insurances, share options, vouchers for food, lunch and holidays, maternity leave crèches, as well as overtime and shift premia are considered, it immediately becomes clear that the non-salary benefits have assumed a greater importance over the recent past than the surveyor might have realised. For accuracy the non-salary benefits should be quantified and then added, although even this is not a foolproof method because some people may not want some of the benefits and some do not apply at all, for example maternity leave.

Within the installation hierarchy there can be as many as twenty different grades and job titles. There are advantages and disadvantages in having a proliferation of titles. As a rule the more job titles that there are, the greater the flexibility of the system. It becomes possible to promote employees without actually promoting them as far as responsibilities or expertise with relation to the job that they are doing are concerned. If this seems unduly cynical, it is not intended to be so. There are instances where a person has been in a job for many years yet is either not suitable for promotion or the system does not allow for advancement. Such a person will either have to change employers or stay and receive only the annual increase unless some provisions are made to re-awaken expectations. On the other hand job titles which give the holder a supervisory job over other staff members when that role does not really exist lead to resentment among the staff if the holder starts to live up to the job title but not the job description or content. Titles such as Team Leader, or the often blessed distinctions between the prefixes Chief and Head, can be the cause of considerable trouble.

By and large, trade unions involved in data-processing demand involvement in the formulation of grading or the changes in grading structures whether these are done by internal mechanisms or by external consultancies. When management consultants first moved into this particular field of personnel and job evaluation most trade unions were hesitant about the techniques used and consequently were compliant even if nominally involved in the process. Times have changed and now all unions can deploy or call upon expertise in these affairs and are in a better position to analyse the faults and mistakes made in other enterprises than either management or the consultants. Providing job evaluation is merely a ranking system, unions generally have little objection to it *per se* but if, as has happened so often in the past, the management takes the opportunity to reduce staffing levels and set immutably external relativities, unions will naturally object. This has occurred in data-processing as in other areas but nowadays unions insist on being involved at the planning stages to pre-empt such unilateral manoeuvres.

Departmentally there are two basic remuneration methods. The first is to pay a single rate for the job; the second is to use incremental scales which in theory represent a payment for experience in that job. In the first case the union merely settles upon a single sum per job grade while, with increments, a range and the progression through the range is negotiated. A variant on either method is to use a 'merit payment' system, either to progress through scales or as a bonus type of supplement. Trade unions generally dislike these systems although some employees are obsessed with them. Secrecy is never a very attractive proposition and merit payments are almost always covert. In this way salary bills are kept to a minimum as it is suggested to individuals that they are getting high merit payments (don't tell the others') while in reality the total sum is small. This covert approach is extended among the smaller computer industry enterprises where there are no published salary scales and thus an internal differential system does not come into the employee's assessment which in turn damps down salary claims and expectations.

At least the training of computer staffs is one area in which a lot of progress has been made. In the past there have been a bewildering variety of courses offered by a very wide group of organisations. Diplomas in various computing techniques are awarded after courses of 6 days or 2 years and we hesitate to suggest that all the people taking the 2-year course were slow learners. The easy availability of training courses gave rise to high staff turnover and also started the difficulties in matching job titles. The 1971 crash saw a re-evaluation of training schemes with the British Computer Society, the Department of Employment and employers setting standards and with the education authorities responding. As a result proper personnel techniques have sometimes replaced the previous random appointments system and the resulting demand and supply pressures have forced a more standardised system. There are still discrepancies, however. *Computer Users' Yearbook 1975* lists many of the courses offered and there are still these marked disparities in time taken to get what should be a standardised qualification, for example Cobol proficiency courses vary from 8 to 40 weeks, and computer appreciation courses from 5 to 52 weeks. When business studies (including computer technique) are included, it is obvious that there is room for not only standardisation but nationalisation. Until such examples disappear by both unions and managements taking action to promote reputable training schemes the gold-rush type of recruitment will remain and work to the disadvantage of all but a small minority.

The first matter that has to be tackled by a union, whether in the computer field or elsewhere is to get recognition. Employers vary as to their response to a request to draw up and sign a procedure agreement; some accept it as inevitable, others challenge the membership figures, others form a staff association, while others just say no. Within the in-house installation staff there has generally been little trouble for trade unions because the enterprises in which such staff are organised have a history of white-collar unionisation. Preceding the recognition the union must of course, have acquired members, but even this must be qualified. It is not unknown for employers to grant recognition to a staff association when that body has less than 10 per cent of the eligible membership and it is also not unknown for employers to grant recognition in outline for a trade union with only one eligible member. This is called a 'sweetheart agreement', and is made with a union with a history of docile behaviour and designed to keep other trade unions out. Such tactics, especially the staff association technique, have been used in the data-processing areas, but only as part of the larger organisation, not as a specifically singled-out department.

Trade-union recruitment in the white-collar sector has created a secondary industry of academic studies, all of which attempt to find the academic's lodestone, the single cause for the membership explosion. Given the changes in the educational system, the increasing percentage size of white-collar employment and the changed area of recruitment the surprise is the slow growth of membership. At one level there is a cut-off point below which membership, if not automatic, comes more easily and this is based less on title or salary level than on future prospects and advancement *vis-à-vis* the internal promotional ladder. Managements, especially in the private sector, are adept at suggesting that union membership represents a division of interest, and that members obviously cannot hold the interests of the organisation close to their bosom. It follows that recruitment is easier where promotion is seen to be more difficult. Career and promotion opportunities are out of reach for 90 per cent of employees in data-processing organisations belonging to larger parent organisations. An administrator on a similar grade and salary to that of a programmer has immeasurably greater opportunities of reaching middle and higher management because the skills employed are in the company's mainstream and not channelled into a speciality. An operator or programmer can at best ultimately expect to be the installation manager, but there is only one of these and perhaps 500 employees and barring accidents and even allowing for academic advancement 499 will be disappointed. It follows that one major barrier to union recruitment is absent in data processing.

There are, however, other barriers. One is by the choice of the union itself. Every union must have an idea of its own cost-effectiveness, even if only intuitively. If a union has 1,000 members split among fifty companies it is immeasurably harder and more expensive to service these than two groups of 500. If, in addition, the problems in the smaller groups are as great as those in the larger groups the union could need twenty-five times as many officials and a proportionate increase in back-up staff – although some economies of scale are possible. These marginal cases therefore, if not actually discouraged, are certainly not encouraged to join a union. The ASTMS whose range of local groups (national negotiations apart) moves from, say, over 3,000 at Rolls-Royce in Derby to three or four in a small west Midland engineering plant, is attempting to solve this problem by the use of its own staff college where it trains lay officials to be able to undertake skilled union representational activities. The smaller institutions like bureaux fall into the hostile category of employees and are another reason why recruitment has been retarded in this field.

A further reason is status. Computer people tend to think of themselves as middle-class professionals, especially from programmers upwards. The feeling is that professional people not only do not need unions, but that to join one is actually an unprofessional act. As a result there have been, although not in the computer case, attempts to form 'professional' unions, mainly among scientists and engineers. As these quasi-unions have foresworn industrial action and also raised severe qualification barriers to membership, it is not surprising to find that they have never 'taken off', and equally predictable that they are welcomed only by the most backward of managements. The basic reason why they fail is that the supposedly professional ethos which does not allow for removal or partial restriction of labour means that, to quote Nye Bevan, they 'go into the council chamber naked'. Not only is their constraint gone and more to the point the employer realises that it has gone, but the ethos that is invoked has nothing whatsoever to do with professional status. No one would deny that doctors are professional men and women yet they withdraw their labour, they refuse to work overtime and generally the British Medical Association acts as a trade union but because of its fundamental lack of expertise in the field rarely entirely satisfies.

The British Computer Society acts as a professional body in a similar manner to the engineering industries. It runs its own examinations and awards qualifications. It has a code of conduct. It encourages discussion, and arranges meetings, on current technology and on the development of the computer sciences. It does not attempt to act as a trade union and cannot remotely be seen as a substitute for an effective one. Providing a person is employed on a salary basis and is subject to dismissal by a person senior to himself or herself and that the remuneration is set by someone other than himself, he or she is not only eligible to join a trade union but regardless of status, should, as precautionary insurance alone, do so. It is only among the 'old-guard' unions that a prejudice against employees with higher status remains – certainly the TUC welcome them. It is interesting that such unions have a miniscule membership in this field while the newer unions, such as ASTMS have a burgeoning membership. Other factors such as performance, image, professional coverage and contributions play their part too, so that it is improper to assert that status is the only reason for this phenomenon of non-unionisation. If union recruitment in the white-collar sector is difficult, the retention of membership is more so. Even if all hostilities are overcome, the members demand a high level of service and approach the union in the same manner as they would a doctor, dentist or accountant, that is as a body which provides expertise which they themselves need to tap. Computer staffs work in a mechanistic environment and have this sort of approach which is understandable and it has to a great degree stimulated the change in expertise levels in British unions over the last few years.

It has been said previously that the reasons for trade-union membership are not exclusively for remuneration increases. The trade union is asked to protect members against redundancies, unfair dismissals, and to advise and represent on changes of work methods and manning levels, to negotiate on job evaluations, to negotiate on health and safety, indeed all in-work environmental matters and to take up individual cases on a variety of subjects. In turn this means that the modern union full-time official has to have knowledge of not only many industries but also much legislation, codes of practice and legal procedures. It is surely no accident that the unions which have the greatest demands made on them in these modern days, the white-collar unions, have with only one exception *appointed* rather than *elected* officials. There are, of course, elected executives controlling union policy, but the introduction of modern industrial and governmental methods into all the facets of labour relations has meant that the election system, where success is often based on factors other than the representation of the members, cannot be relied upon to throw up full-time officials capable of coping with the situation.

This is, however, not all that a union needs to provide. It must keep members informed about not only their own industry but the union's general work and to do this it has to set up and administer liaison committees, ensure a regular supply of printed material concerning organisation and policy reaches the branches and provide a journal. There are legal departments, research departments, education departments, pensions experts, health and safety experts and a host of others whose expertise can be tapped at short notice when required. It is, in a modern union, a formidable array of talent but an array which is needed to match the expertise of employers and the Government. Even this is not all. A large part of a trade union's work is to lobby on behalf of members about the industries in which they work and on behalf of members and their families on points – social and political – which are delineated by the regular Conferences of the union, as well as coping with incomes policies.

Representations to Government on behalf of an industry are more difficult since UK accession to the EEC because so many decisions are taken *de facto* in the Commission. Unions then, such as ASTMS, now need to have a Parliamentary Committee which will meet regularly and discuss methods of raising certain points which are of concern to the membership. These can be concerned with employment, profitability, proposed legislation or legislation in the committee stage or social, moral or political questions. Discussions and action have covered items as diverse as nuclear reactors, abortion, pension legislation, computer manufacturing, the National Health Service and MPs' salaries. The computer manufacturing industry is one area where a great number of meetings have been set up with Ministers and questions persistently and repeatedly asked in the House.

The main computer manufacturers in the United Kingdom between them employ 41,800 staff in all (September 1975), a reduction from the high point in 1972. Of these manufacturers, both of the hard-ware and peripherals, the ones who employ the most are International Computers (ICL), International Business Machines (IBM), Burroughs, Honeywell, Elliot (GEC), Ferranti and Univac. The Americans control most of the world market in computers, mainly though by no means exclusively through IBM, while Britain is one of only two countries in the world, the other is Japan, where indigenous-based companies have over 50 per cent of the market.

The major British company is ICL which manufactures both large and mini-computers with some success. It is, however, a very vulnerable company in that it has to compete directly with the giant American-owned corporations which have the advantage of large corporate finances to research, develop, and sell new products. The annual research and development budget of IBM is greater than the total annual revenue of ICL which gives some indication of the size of opposition the British-owned company faces. Trade unions have several good reasons for wanting ICL to continue production.

If that production were to cease, the demand for computers would be met by foreign companies (basically American). Some of these would be manufactured abroad thus, in total, decreasing employment in Britain and adding to the balance of payments deficit. Even if all the residual equipment was manufactured in Britain, it is unlikely that more than half of the ICL staff would be re-employed by competitors. In addition, successive balance of payments deficits have ultimately forced British governments to deflate the economy, to restrict wages and to create unemployment – the stop in our regular stop–go cycle. Obviously unions will resist anything which adds to the deficit in jobs.

Well before 1971 it was obvious that ICL and its predecessor companies would not only need Government assistance but also some form of central government preference in ordering if it were to survive. Central government accounts for roughly 18 per cent of all computer revenue in Britain and ICL has 56 per cent of the sales and 40 per cent of the hiring revenue from this source. It is biased towards the larger machines rather than minicomputers. In 1975/76 this accounted for £31.7 million. Unions have long pressed for local government and government agencies to use ICL equipment but with varying degrees of success. In 1971 when the industry had its abrupt decline ICL needed capital and Government growth and loans were made available after (but not necessarily because of) intensive lobbying by the interested trade union to the Department of Industry. ICL's subsequent success, including the production of new ranges of large and small computers, can perhaps be measured by the fact that all of the Government monies available to it were not taken up. This was despite the unfavourable economic climate prevailing at the time (1971).

There are, however, many British major public sector organisations which make use of non-ICL basic equipment. In the education and research, local government, public corporations and central government sectors there are at least fifty of which over thirty are IBM. These users include the Atomic Weapons Research Establishment, the Meteorological Office, several universities (including London), the Greater London Council, the Post Office, British Steel, Gas and Electricity Boards, the Metropolitan Police, the Central Statistics Office and oddly enough the Scottish Office Computer Service itself. It does seem strange that the Government, committed as it is to a viable British-owned computer industry allows such a major segment to pass into foreign-owned hands.

During 1975 ICL made employees redundant – including many in Research and Development – and the fear is that far from expanding it is being prepared to become a marketing operation only. There are reasonable grounds for such fears. This strategy would only be a reflection of the wider British run-down of manufacturing industry. Before Britain entered the EEC pressure was put on for ICL to merge with a European-based federation of manufacturers and this went as far as a Commission official giving evidence to this effect to a House of Commons Select Committee. The disturbing feature of this was that the merger was overtly for political reasons and not on technological or commercial grounds. It was fortunately rejected. Several American-based consortia have been interested in ICL and either a European or North American arrangement, stopping short of a merger but switching new production out of Britain, is still possible and the cutting of Research and Development, which is, after all, only future production, is most disturbing. The magnitude of the problem is shown by the import penetration figures for the United Kingdom in the computer sub-section which at 1974 stood at 70 per cent. Such a merger would naturally be opposed by British unions to the extent of industrial action if necessary but it is obvious that ICL as it stands at present may not be a long-term viable concern.

Its base is far too narrow. Most other computer manufacturers have a wider range of productions based on electronics and also have wider markets. ICL will have to acquire such a base, if necessary through acquisition by the National Enterprise Board or by a merger with another British manufacturer, for example, GEC Elliot or with a company such as Ferranti under the aegis of the National Enterprise Board. It would be disastrous for British technology if ICL were to close. Successive governments have paid lip service to the idea of a high-value-added, high technological industrial base and computers are a growing and vital part of such a system. Given its narrow range (it almost disappears when viewed sideways on) the company is overly vulnerable to changes in the prevailing economic climate; a Government expenditure cut may, for example, lead to the cancellation of one or more large machines and this in itself would create considerable difficulties. One further problem of ICL leaving the market is what happens when a foreign-owned multi-national company takes over. Honeywell made many employees in Scotland redundant and the work that they did was transferred to Honeywell plants overseas with the British market maintained.

Trade unions represent employees within the computer manufacturing industry as they do employees in any industry, although one major difference is the very low percentage of manual and skilled manual workers who are members. Thus, most unusually for a manufacturing company, the largest union is non-manual. There are procedure agreements for 'white-' and 'blue-collar' unions at ICL, Burroughs, Honeywell, Elliot, Ferranti and there will soon be one at Univac, but one company refuses to negotiate and that is IBM. IBM behaves like some other multi-national companies (Michelin is another example) in having a global anti-union corporate policy. What such companies do, and it is a time-honoured union-resistant technique, is to allow membership of a union but to deny any facilities (notice board use for example) until there is recognition. This tolerance by the company of individual membership will continue until it reaches a critical point in a department, let us say 30 per cent. At this time the company will embark on an anti-union offensive, letters, circulars, notice-boards, even enclosures in salary notifications generally pointing out not only the irrelevance of a trade union but also the dangers of a trade union and, in some of the messages of trade-union membership, to the individual. When the union puts in a claim for recognition it is refused. If a ballot or audit is forced then the constituency is widened sufficiently to dilute percentage membership. All the time the company trades on the fact that industrial action will not be taken, or, if taken, will collapse very quickly. If there is no recognition, there is no point in being a member of the union and so employees resign membership of the union and about 2 years later the cycle starts all over again. Generally speaking employees will not join a trade union and pay its subscription (low in relation to income though it may be) if no service is forthcoming. That would be like buying a colour TV licence when you have no television set.

The Employment Protection Act with its recognition procedures and the Advisory, Conciliation and Arbitration Service (ACAS) which is part and parcel of that Act plus the definition of independent unions may well change this sorry state of affairs.

A computer manufacturing company presents problems to trade unions totally different from those presented by the installations. To start with, there is a far wider cross-section of employees; ICL alone have over 100 job titles. These are divided between the actual manufacturing departments which themselves will be broken down into sub-departments, a sales force, a service department, installation employees, and a Research and Development department and behind all of these are the clerical and administrative staffs.

The annual salary negotiation may be carried out by each individual union separately on behalf of its members or it may negotiate in a joint-union committee. There may be site negotiations, certainly for individual grievances and disciplinary matters and there may be separate negotiations for each group of members. There is, under normal circumstances, little identification between service engineers and research technicians in respect of job content, and negotiations regarding remuneration are supposed partially to reflect this factor. A strange relationship has been built up in the computer manufacturing industry in that for some of the time the unions and management act in concert when cajoling government and for the remainder of the time they are in conflict over the industrial relations of the company.

As yet unions have not gained much of a foothold in the peripheral manufacturing industry. The industry is new and the units are small and the employees pushing forward the frontiers of technology are too enthralled to need trade-union support, rather like many small voluntary agency workers. If this industry, and indeed the manufacturing industry itself, develops as general technology develops then this situation will change. In industrial terms computer manufacturing is a cottage industry, small and inefficient but, with its hoped-for growth, will have to come new industrial relations techniques, more professionalism and less of the amateur spirit. In this respect it is rather like the motor-car manufacturing companies before Henry Ford's application of the production line. Finally, what unions will want now are Planning Agreements.

Planning Agreements would enable employees to have both information about and participation within the industry. The industry itself is volatile but is capable of *leading* technological change rather than responding to it. Agreements reached with the Department of Industry with trade-union participation can not only tap the hitherto neglected reservoir of talent and ideas within the labour force, but convince the employees of the companies and indeed employees in all walks of life that living can change for the better. If the unions are the one stabilising force in the installations sector they can be a more positive force in the manufacturing sector. In a world trade context our future may well depend on computer people and these people need a stake in their development and the only organisations capable of providing this stake are the trade unions.

Chapter 8

Bargaining digitally

People often complain they are the victim of taxes, yet when it is pointed out what they get in return for those taxes – health services, pensions, roads, schools, safety, indeed the whole social infrastructure – they often change the discussion. So it is with computers. People dislike and fear the dehumanisation, the science fiction story inexorably becoming true and seize avidly on the widely publicised mistakes and reminisce about the pre-computer days when bacon was crisper, sixpence (2½p) could buy a pint of beer, a packet of cigarettes and a trip to the music hall and you could still get change left over. People forget the inconvenience, the poverty, the unemployment, the drudgery and the infant mortality rate, yet rather like removing the services provided by taxes, removing the services of the computer would whistle up a storm of protest about living standards and consumer convenience. Unions are often in this invidious position themselves, complaining about the effects of the computer yet enjoying its fruits.

The computer can not only make life easier for a trade union in running its internal affairs, it can also facilitate union negotiations; in fact one could argue that certain benefits would be impossible without the aid of computers. As unions are now interested in almost all aspects of the modern world and computers are involved in these self-same aspects there is obviously a strong link between computers and unions doing their everyday business. However, the connection goes somewhat deeper than this in many respects.

The basic facility of the computer, that of retaining an immense amount of information, and its ability to classify and then retrieve that information can be of great assistance to unions. On the other hand it can be said that computers are put to some uses merely to justify the existence of the computer. This is rather similar to the decade of the 1960s when managements acquired installations and then thought of things that could be done with them.

A union needs to store information for bargaining purposes and this is usually done in its Research Department, although in some unions there is a separate Condition or Movements Department. The information required varies quite considerably as between different types of negotiation and different industries and it is necessary to distinguish between them and the opinions of union officials concerning them. The type of information to be stored and the way it is stored and retrieved will depend on the number and type of negotiations undertaken.

Basically, certain statistics are needed to back up a salary or conditions claim or perhaps to argue against a management statement. These will generally centre around data for comparable groups of employees in the same industry, represented by the same union; data on comparable groups in the industry represented by other unions, or indeed non-unionised; data on comparable groups in other industries; data on internal differentials; data on corporate profits (if applicable); data on retail price index, other indices, average earnings and a multiplicity of other facts depending on the circumstances. Given that this sort of data is required, is it always needed and is it always available?

The first point is that it is not always needed, indeed some trade unionists would argue that it is not needed at all. The argument is that managements seldom if ever listen to logical argument; that they have an upper limit on the amount they are prepared to pay; will try to get acceptance for a smaller amount and that industrial action is the only argument a management will move on. The sophisticated argument then points out that many consultancies provide managements with the salary levels they should pay, given their job evaluation, and that debate over this level is useless. There is, sad to say, weight in these views; management in Britain has historically seen its function as a cost minimising one and detailed arguments and figures are met with a polite 'I hear what you say but . . .' type of reply. However, even if this scenario holds there are imperatives for providing a well-documented claim; these are firstly that trade unionism should be seen to take the rational viewpoint and secondly to convince the members themselves that they have fallen behind in order to get the industrial action needed to explode the management's prior value judgements. Contrary to widely-held beliefs it can be very difficult to get British employees to take any action unless they are convinced of the injustices perpetuated by the management side.

Typically negotiations are locally staged and are on behalf of members in one plant at one location. By far the majority of negotiations are of this type although in terms of the numbers of people involved they represent less than 50 per cent of the total. This type of negotiation generally only uses local comparisons in comparable industries and such data is often available in the local union offices. The second type of negotiation is the national one where all plants and divisions are bound by the same negotiation and this may be conducted between a single employer, as in the insurance industry, or a federation such as the Engineering Employers Federation. The latter case often also has a joint-union panel on the other side and typically the negotiations only set minimum rates with local 'top-ups' coming later. Obviously in such cases national data is used (or international for holidays), but if an industry rather than a company is involved, the data is generally from a different industry.

The third negotiating method is the direct comparison and can scarcely be called a negotiation at all. In such cases, the Civil Service Pay Research Unit is an example, pre-selected jobs and industries are used to provide an 'outside' salary level and thus the Civil Service level of pay. The Pay Unit itself rather than the unions undertakes to provide the comparisons, although in other similar forms of pay setting there is no third party assistance.

Unions vary in their membership and the type of negotiations in which they are involved. The public sector unions are most often involved in national-level negotiations and consequently the internal information is limited in amount, easy to handle, store and retrieve. At the other end of the spectrum are unions with members in both the private and public sectors, with both domestic and national negotiations. Unions such as the TGWU, the EETPU and ASTMS fit into this category. Information here can run, as in the case of ASTMS, into at least 5,500 different groups each with different characteristics. These are internal information sources. The external sources are diffuse, difficult to gather and erratic. As the salary rankings between jobs and industries are continually being adjusted it is not possible to narrow down the number of external comparators. Merely looking at the Department of Employment industrial classification with twenty-six very broad categories and then realising that on top of this there needs to be a job breakdown, will indicate the scope of the problem. Other data such as the Retail Price Index, average earnings and other Government data are easily available.

In a domestic negotiation primarily only local rates will be acceptable and these will be available (at least the internal ones) to the local union office, and the liaison between this office and other local union offices is probably more likely than the Head Office Research Departments to produce local external comparators. Many officials at local level do not trouble Research Departments for salary data because their own sources are that much better. In a national-level negotiation most of the salary comparisons will come from outside the industry, unless for example the negotiation is on behalf of one insurance company, in which case other companies' salary levels may well be cited; most national-level negotiations, however, are on behalf of industries themselves and thus intra-industry comparators are inappropriate except for new national standard setting in the conditions area. Finally the pre-selected comparator negotiation requires little work in that there is a fixed and finite list which is easily stored and retrieved.

For a trade union with many thousands of different agreements per year, both national and domestic and covering a very wide spectrum of industry and commerce, there are then three questions to be asked: can all the information be centrally stored?; if so how often will it be used?; how useful will this be in any event? If it is decided that centrally stored information is both useful and practicable then obviously a computer is the storage receptacle of choice. For example, is it useful for a union to know how many data-processing staff it has in membership? From the point of view of a union such as ASTMS this would not help negotiate a single salary, it might conceivably help in recruitment, it would not help in administration; in other words such a statistic would be of only the most marginal value.

Even if it were decided that agreements should be stored centrally using a computer, there is still the cost problem. Computer costs are high, but often existing overheads are even higher and it pays to change to computers. If a union makes a great number of agreements per year and many of these are local, and if coordinating (combine) negotiating committees monitor these agreements with some agreements also at Head Office, there is obviously a duplication of information problem and a wastage of money, both directly and indirectly, in labour costs. These costs must be more in aggregate than the extra cost of using computer time if a financial benefit is to be felt, or to be very fair the costs plus and imputed benefit derived from increased efficiency. To get an idea of costs one must first look at an agreement, what it contains and how it relates to others.

An agreement is reached between the employer and union and for the sake of simplicity let us assume that it deals with salaries alone. There may be one, there may be 100 different grades. Each grade may have a different salary level or range of salary levels, a different progression within the range, different hours of work and different overtime and shift premia. Without job titles that information is useless, job titles without job descriptions makes it suspect. A foreman supervising five hands cannot strictly be compared with one supervising twenty and some rather strict coding will have to be used. Equally it would be possible to code and fragment all money income. However, over a wide range of different industries (about forty in the case of ASTMS) and the public sector in addition, the number of different variables needed starts to get quite out of hand. It would be possible to cut down those by ignoring certain distinctions, but the more this is done the more inaccurate or generalised the resulting information becomes. One essential rule in negotiations with an employer where a written claim has been prepared is never make a mistake, never leave an opening into which an employer can insert a knife and twist. This rule continues: if facts can be disputed, leave them out. The cost of a full retrieval service would be somewhat prohibitive, with forty industries, about 18,000 different job titles and descriptions or about 75,000 different basic salary levels. This is what the ASTMS internal information would entail and this does not take into account changing earnings for fringe benefits. It also does not take into account the external information problem.

It is obviously desirable to have the best and most efficient system possible. Ideally every time an agreement is concluded, the information should be entered into specially prepared cards and sent to head office. These would be punched up and stored and then, when an official needs information he could request say, salaries for supervisors in federated engineering companies in Norfolk and Suffolk, supervising a stated range of shop-floor workers all with salaries above a certain level. Hopefully, the computer via the operators would do the necessary. One could go further and suggest a terminal in each local office bypassing head office staff and allowing local officials and staff direct access, even with a real-time system if desirable.

The second alternative is to have a central union data-bank of agreements, maintained either by the TUC or by an entirely new service body. This would have many opponents in the trade-union movement, however. Proportional secrecy is still endemic in bargaining and for such a bank to be successful unions would have to have access to other unions' information and might find, in passing, that some unions had been poaching on fenced preserves. The problem of security would be great and, of course, one would not like a Government to have access especially in an incomes policy period backed by statute.

Why court problems? We come back to the point as to whether such detailed claims are in fact useful in themselves, leaving aside the budgetary constraints. For an ordinary claim, probably not, at least not until the time when employers not only listen but attend genuinely prepared to be convinced. Most unions do have financial constraints and a comprehensive system would be out of reach of most given the present number and structure of unions. This would reinforce the argument against the present use of such systems. However, neglecting internal administrative functions, ordinary negotiations are not the only issue in which computers could play a part in trade union activities.

Each year a relatively high number of negotiations end with an arbiter settling the issue and, with the emergence of the ACAS, referred to in the previous chapter, it would not be surprising if this number were to increase. Arbitrations differ from negotiations in one vital respect. In a negotiation it is often pointless to use information to persuade as the employer has a pre-conceived position; in an arbitration the whole purpose is to provide information to an impartial third party in order to persuade. This changes the whole emphasis to one of the collection and presentation of data. This must be accurate and relevant, there can be no recourse to outside help except those bodies that aid trade unions from time to time, such as the Labour Research Department and the Ruskin College unit; equally, there is little chance of industrial action to retrieve the situation should mistakes be made. In such circumstances the maintenance of good records and the computer's ability to analyse them quickly and accurately would be invaluable. If this part of industrial relations grows quickly, and the idea behind the formation of the ACAS is that it should, then the stimulus for computer-aided research by unions will be considerably strengthened.

On the other side of the negotiating table, both individual employers and employers' federations use computers for bargaining. This use can take two forms. The first is the collection of commercial and other data about the company to prove, say, how badly it is doing, how overmanned it is and how another £1 per week increase will drive it into the hands of the receiver. This tactic now sanctified by time in our oldest companies, gains credence if reams of computer print-out are produced for dramatic effect to make some point or other during negotiations. The second use is for salary comparisons. If anyone knows what salaries are being paid it is the employer and the larger federations maintain a data-bank of salaries and earnings within their jurisdiction. Although there is the potent argument that, if the employers use a technique then unions should match it, it must be pointed out firstly that employers have considerably more money and secondly that they already have installations and probably have spare capacity on them.

Employers need the computer in bargaining for one other reason. The remuneration package is not constant across the organisation; there are still sex differences, age differences and status differences. If an employer is faced with a claim involving six elements he will have to cost them before responding to the claim and determining his side of the trade-off. Without a computer staffing schedule and a quickly obtainable picture of who receives what, this could be an impossible task. The growth of the remuneration package does seem to have coincided with the growth in computer use and although there is probably no direct connection the package concept would probably not exist if the computer were not there to work out both the allocations and costs and to administer the various schemes. The latest in the line of packages is the 'shopping basket approach' where benefits can be changed as circumstances change within the constraint of a global sum. For example a young financial executive might opt for a school fees provision for his children (certainly most unions would not negotiate such a benefit) and when he is older prefer to switch this expenditure to share options. Obviously this sort of arrangement needs a computer even more than the conventional once and for all type of package.

The future is of more than passing speculation to trade unions. They are continuing bodies. They need to know, but rarely get the chance to know, the future prospects of the economy, industry and the individual enterprise. Some unions try to predict what might happen, privately and publicly to the economy, but apart from the National Economic Development Office analyses there is no information on sectoral changes available. Where company level predictions are concerned, about the last people informed are the employees and their trade unions. To some extent this should now change as a result of recent legislation. Two Parliamentary Acts are concerned. The first is the Employment Protection Act which states that unions should be given information by managements so that they may conduct their collective bargaining from a position of knowledge. For this purpose the ACAS has been charged with producing a list of what may reasonably be required. The second is the Industry Act which has two relevant sections. The first section also concerns disclosure of information provisions though not necessarily to aid bargaining but to inform the work-force of what the prospects are in their company. The second section concerns the Planning Agreement which potentially at least will have the greatest impact.

Apart from the fact that employers, when giving the information, will have to make use of their computers, there is little a union can do to process the information given; it has to be taken on trust. The Planning Agreement is, however, somewhat different. As originally conceived it was to be an Agreement between the enterprise and the appropriate government department with the appropriate trade unions having an input into both sides. At the time of writing there has yet to be an Agreement and it is difficult to say that there will ever be an adequate text. The Agreement will be based on a rolling plan, probably 5 years but depending on the planning cycle of the company, and will try to estimate the investment rate, manpower requirements, sales, etc., over this period. This is a complete reversal of roles for trade unions in that for the first time it will be possible for them to break out of the short-term reactive role in which they have been trapped. This does, however, pose serious problems with the major one being of expertise in handling data.

The main danger will be that trade unionists will be put into the position of mere information receivers, unable to challenge the data presented to them because of its technical nature. Computers will of course play a large part in the forecasting, or rather should play a large part. Information from NEDO on the sectoral prospects, and from Whitehall on national and international prospects will be combined with the company's own analysis of its prospects. To do this there must be a sophisticated set of calculations based on this data and assumptions made by all three bodies, and such calculations can really only be made using the facilities offered by a computer.

When the information is presented to trade unions they will be faced with three distinct problems. The first is the form in which the information is presented – for few trade unionists are yet skilled at interpreting print-outs and one suspects (perhaps unjustly) that information could be presented in the most baffling way possible, trading on the assumption that few people want to admit their ignorance. Another problem will be to understand the information even if it is presented in a comprehensible form. It will certainly involve some considerable amount of technical forecasting and few union members have expertise in investment analysis, market research, etc. Finally and probably the most important is the question of what assumptions have been made.

Computer forecasting, as with other methods, depends totally on the assumptions made in the model and the variables that have been included or excluded, and if there is to be any challenge to the results it is in this area that the challenge must be made. For example Treasury economic forecasting has been, to understate the matter, patchy and inadequate over the years yet it employs very competent economists and uses computers, so the problem must lie in the assumptions that they use in their models. If trade unionists are to participate fully in Planning Agreements they must be in a position to challenge assumptions, variables, and conclusions; the alternative will be for them to act as a rubber stamp, legitimising unpalatable decisions for public relations purposes.

One of the authors of this book attended a seminar for the benefit of a major computer manufacturer in which the capacity of its products to frame an analysis of the future was extolled. But it turned out, this was based on the assumptions that;

(i) That there would be no Third World War;
(ii) Middle East tension would continue;
(iii) The EEC would stagnate;
(iv) Surreptitious Japanese import controls would continue.

Who set this frame of reference? Not the computer system: it seems to have been a human intelligence in Colorado named Fred!

Nearly all Planning Agreements will involve many unions for only the larger companies will be involved. As considerable training will be needed and as considerable work will need to be done it would appear illogical for many unions to duplicate each others' work and it is doubtful whether any one union could cope with the work load. Training in computer appreciation, economics and business studies needs to be undertaken quickly but even this does not go far enough.

There is probably a need for a National Research Centre staffed by experts, but under the control of trade unions and business. This would provide an independent assessment of the conclusions of Planning Agreements and rework basic data using computers, if necessary, using different assumptions and variables. There is also no reason why such an agency should not be able to produce politically-independent sectoral, national and international economic forecasts. The trade-union movement in Britain has been quick to demand, but slow to press, for better information on behalf of its members. If information is given it should be of benefit to both sides of industry because decisions taken in the light of information are generally more rational than those where speculation rules the day. It is unfair to ask trade unions to exercise responsibility if neither participation nor information are made available to them; that is merely to perpetuate the role of the employee as victim, and in a Planning Agreement system as a willing victim.

As yet, few unions use computers for negotiating purposes or for any purpose other than administration, partly on the grounds of cost and partly on grounds of usefulness. However, as unions and members become more involved in decision-making processes and as the inevitable rationalisation of both industries and unions proceeds, computer-use will become necessary. Trade unions must avoid the pitfalls of an installation which simply looks like conspicuous consumption, and of using it to perform tasks which are peripheral to organisational needs. Industry and commerce made these mistakes and it was costly; the trade unions must learn from these mistakes.

Chapter 9

More or less jobs

There is a widely held and rosy view of a future where most jobs will have been replaced by automated techniques which will then release us all from the drudgery of work to live our lives in style, luxury and leisure. There is also a view of the future which is rather more sombre, a study in blue, where computers have become our masters and we all work in a technologically inspired state of total boredom. Both views have their fervent admirers and detractors; neither view is provable, but neither can be dismissed. It would be easy to say that the truth must lie somewhere in-between – the responsible moderate position, but unfortunately, as in politics, such a position although superficially attractive is invariably wrong. As we progress down the road to automation so society will have to question exactly where it is going and for what purpose; certainly, computer people are not yet really doing so.

In Britain we have a poor record of taking the long view and a pretty poor one when considering the medium-term prospects in social, political or economic affairs. This would seem to be particularly so for those who spend their lives close to the subject under discussion; the proximity seems to induce a state of enchantment with trivia, often technological, and distaste for anything outside of this.

Fortunately those of us on the outside looking in, the overwhelming majority of the population, have a history within the UK of not accepting the role of passive victim. The computer has affected us all as consumers, as employees, and the changes that it has wrought are the concern of us all. Obviously concern, if it is to be made public, and/or effective, must be channelled through and amplified by an organisation. This may be an *ad hoc* one set up for a particular purpose, for example, the Stansted Airport Protest Committee, or it may be one which already exists and has a permanent standing in the matter, such as a trade union. From the union point of view its members have to be represented for the short-term contingencies that arise and among these are redundancies, some of which may be due to the installation of a computer.

We have illustrated, in an earlier chapter, on how work patterns can be changed and how technological redundancy or boredom can develop. Ever since the Spinning Jenny, new technological developments have been the subject of gloom and doom prognostications about the effect their introduction will have on the quality of life and on employment prospects. The computer has probably spawned more of this thinking than any other single piece of equipment, yet – and this is the most surprising thing – the employment situation has not worsened as noticeably as was feared and this requires some explanation. The phenomenon is not just confined to Britain. The USA has shown the same lack of expected reaction, so it is not merely a national structural phenomenon.

The computer is a very different innovation from others in that its scope and abilities are capable of wider exploitation – across industries, across continents and even across space – than other inventions. This is well known and the benefits have been promised over the years, yet as with the lack of net unemployment resulting so the potential has not been anything like realised. One reason for the lack of technological redundancies is this under use of the computer, or to be accurate its use in the non-productive sectors. The feature film has not lived up to the trailer.

A standing rebuke in the computer world is the installation which was put in to save money and salaries but ended up with the enterprise employing more people. It is not exactly a joke and is another reason why unemployment has not been as high as was feared. Not only does an installation need staff, but people are needed to receive and program the information in such a form that the computer can be used and only too often this has meant an increase in the total number of people who have had to be employed. The installation has, however, probably made more people redundant overall. If, as is so widely done, the computer takes care of the salaries, tax, pensions, invoices and bills, those departments will have been made redundant. Yet in net terms total employment may remain constant. This does not mean that those who had the jobs originally will have the new jobs, although some will have been retrained and retained. The computer in fact stimulates job changes in such circumstances, with a high change-over of staff within the enterprise.

There are many jobs which computers theoretically can eliminate but still exist. The professions – medicine, dentistry, accountancy and the law – all employ expertise which is deployed and modified by the individual using his or her experiences. This is something the computer is not capable of duplicating, neither at present nor in the foreseeable future where the cost of attempting it would be prohibitive. At the other end of the scale many manual jobs such as sweeping and cleaning, and cooking, are not replaceable by computer. In between there is the vast range of clerical, administrative, scientific and manufacturing jobs which could partially be replaced, but which in the present state of computer technology have not even been the subject of research. Nevertheless, there have been some redundancies and these have been in the clerical and administrative and the shop-floor areas.

It is among the skilled operatives that jobs have been the most threatened. The numerically controlled machine and the automatic welding devices have made many craftsmen obsolete while the unskilled or semi-skilled manual operative is still in demand to look after machines or work on production tracks. Clerical and administrative workers have been superseded by installations although as we have pointed out, other routine work often appears to take its place. There are, however, also indirect redundancy effects due to company mergers (and occasionally job mergers) which, in a sense, have been brought about by the computer, and further indirect effects when a changed process offsets a supplier industry or service. The process is piecemeal, plant by plant, office by office – nothing is planned outside the immediate installation. It is a wearing down by the drip method rather than a cataract since the time taken to reflect the redundancies is quite long. We are really little further towards any realisation of either of the two long-term views of society, although it is now thought that the decade of the 1970s will start to see the fulfilment of the promise of the 1960s and in turn this will mean increasing technological redundancy.

The trade-union movement has, as we stated earlier, been singularly ineffective when dealing with the industrial effects of the computer in many respects, but it actually may have been more narrowly effective in some areas than at first meets the eye. The devotion to the Parkinsonian theory of data processing shown by much of British management may have been stimulated by the union. Certainly the sectors where a build-up of labour has taken place, notably local and central Government, are also the areas where there has been the greatest penetration of trade unions. These unions have always reserved their greatest militancy for the problem of redundancy and have managed, through successive re-organisations, to increase rather than decrease their total number of members. The reason why the computer has made little if any unemployment impact in these areas may be due to the ethos of the particular unions.

However, this is a singularly non-provable hypothesis and the major impression is still one of reactive struggle rather than pre-emptive action. It could, of course, be argued that instead of redundancies a form of tacit work-sharing has arisen and the hours worked per week have fallen, but there is no evidence that any such movements have been directly connected to the installation of a computer. There are signs, however, that unions are coming to terms with the computer and are starting to protect their members in potentially difficult situations in a variety of ways. This protection may, but need not necessarily, be the continuation of employment even though the job has disappeared. Unions no longer act as twentieth-century technological ostriches. There are other methods available, for example, retraining, enhanced labour mobility or direction of labour and direct public investment programmes. However, it must be stated at once that the British political and social systems mitigate against their success.

The first task for a union is to get information about an impending installation or automated technique. This is not the company hand-out but a detailed analysis of what it seems to effect in the short term; what it might do in the medium and long terms; how many people will be employed; how many made redundant; how many will have job transformations. Once this information has been received, analysed and discussed with the affected membership, talks open with management on cooperation between the parties in getting a smooth transition to the new system. The union always has a good bargaining position in that not only is such an installation an expensive operation but it generally also has members in other departments on whose 'goodwill' the data-processing department will depend.

If an in-house computer is being installed a trade union will want one or more of the following conditions met, depending on the circumstances. No redundancy whatsoever, retraining and continued employment of existing staff, voluntary redundancy or early retirement schemes, a halt to the advertising of new jobs, enhanced redundancy payments, productivity schemes, some sort of selected redundancy system and promotional salary guarantees.

From the members' point of view no redundancy whatsoever is the most desirable position because even though there are always a few who would willingly go, the union has to take the slightly longer view with regard to the total establishment and promotion. There are in existence a few important 'no involuntary redundancy' agreements, and in such cases all members are covered. In any event, whether or not some people are going the unions will ask for the retraining of those staff at risk (who wish to be retrained), either to work within the new data-processing department or in some other department of the same enterprise. If, at the end of a satisfactory training period or, if no training is offered and there is just redeployment within the organisation, it is necessary for the employee to have assistance with house selling and purchases, removal, schooling for children and visiting expenses, etc., the union will expect it all to be provided by the employer.

Most often some people are made redundant when they are either not suitable for, or do not want retraining and their skills are too specific to be of use in other departments. In these cases the unions will want as a first choice a voluntary redundancy scheme, or in cases of people within 10 years of normal retirement age a voluntary early retirement scheme. In both of these cases, as well as in a normal redundancy situation the union will want the member to leave through a money-shaped exit with enhanced redundancy payments and pensions. There are excellent examples of such agreements for ordinary employees in Britain, not in the same league as the quarter-million pound golden handshakes identified with failed senior executives, but both substantial lump sum and pension payments have been negotiated.

Not unnaturally in any situation where redundancy is in the offing the union will expect both new recruitment and job advertising to stop. It is surprising how many times a company will, on the one hand suggest that redundancy among existing staff is inevitable and on the other will recruit new staff. If a union is convinced that redundancies are inevitable and that early retirement or voluntary redundancy are impracticable then it will have to accede to some form of formalised scheme, generally LIFO (Last In, First Out). The union members' attitude will obviously vary depending on whether there is other employment easily available; so one would expect less resistance in a time of relative economic boom and far more in a slump, while there will also be regional differences to take into account.

Two other points will exercise the union in such a situation. The first is the attempt to guarantee not only existing but future salaries and career progression, though the latter may well be impossible given the inevitable change in organisation that takes place. The second is the arrangement of some measure by which any increased productivity gains can be passed on to the remaining staff. Quite often a reduced number of staff end up having to work harder even though the computer was supposed to have made their former colleagues' jobs redundant and in these circumstances unions will feel it unreasonable that such work should go unrewarded. The major point for a trade union to bear in mind is that the employer will often want people to go and thus the onus must be on the employer to make leaving as attractive as possible. Most union members will take some form of action over redundancy situations and employers know this. Union members equally know that the concept behind the introduction of a computer is, at least in the private sector, to increase profits and they feel that such an increase cannot be totally at the expense of the work-force, hence the willingness to take action if needs be.

Somewhat different situations exist where numerically controlled machines or automated production processes are introduced. The controlled machine has made skilled craftsmen redundant, with one machine being capable of doing identical work, to a continuously high standard, many times more quickly than the craftsman. In some of these cases the unions concerned have negotiated agreements whereby the machines are 'minded' by a skilled man where the skill is needed in case of breakdowns. However, as far fewer men are needed alongside a greater output there has been an increasing level of technological redundancy in this area. Automated production techniques come into two categories. The first is the almost totally-computer-controlled process where a handful of men plus the machines have taken the place of hundreds of men. The second is the more efficient use of the productive process which may not actually lead to redundancy but may lead to faster track speed and higher productivity per employee. The first instance has not been satisfactorily dealt with in Britain partly owing to the fact that the new plant does not immediately supersede the old method; for some time the two run in parallel and the best that can be done is to run down the existing procedure by natural wastage and redeployment within the enterprise. The second automated method is more a question of piece rates or measured day-work rates and will be dealt with later in the book.

One basic and fundamental problem underlines this whole subject and that is the lack of mobility of labour in Britain (both between skills and geographically) and the structural disincentives to mobility. If we look at examples of technological redundancies in the white-collar sector they have basically been in banking, insurance and shipping, and in all these the skills needed in the original jobs have been capable of transferring to local authorities or other growth areas. However, the printing industry is quite another matter. Here, especially in the national newspaper section new automated techniques will make a high percentage of existing skilled staff redundant; their skills are not transferable and furthermore the retraining facilities, especially in the London area, are not capable of coping. Strangely enough the advent of the mini-computer and silicon chips may well make a high percentage of both operating and manufacturing staffs redundant in the near future in the computer industry itself. Chips are the latest but probably not the last of the technological advances in computer electronics and will replace circuitory and transistors as readily as transistors and printed circuits replaced the valve and its cumbersome wiring. In all these circumstances what can such staff do?

Britain does not have even a reasonable retraining programme. Either the facilities are not available, or where some exist the courses offered are inadequate. On top of this the housing system in Britain mitigates against geographical movement. If a family lives in rented municipal accommodation and has to move it is almost certain that they will go to the bottom of their new housing list and face a long wait. The alternative is generally high-cost renting or prohibitively high-cost, high-interest rate house purchase. If the family is leaving their own home in a depressed area to move to a more prosperous area a considerable loss will be made on the transaction and unless the new salary is much higher, and this is a promotion and not a redundancy situation, the move will not be possible.

Computer installing needs planning, but so does coping with the effects of the installation and this is one facet that has been conspicuously neglected. Although one reason for this is the lack of hard information about the consequences which is available, the major reason is that computers are introduced on a local basis, each installation being discrete. The repercussions, however, cannot be dealt with on the same level; the ripple effects may include a different industry, or even a different sector of the economy; the effects may be in a totally different geographical area. It follows that if we wish to have a policy which will minimise all the undesirable side-effects it must involve a radical approach to the problem. As there is no way of dealing with such problems across industries or across companies because there is no mechanism which allows for the liaison necessary, we either have to shrug our shoulders and accept the inevitable, or draw up such a mechanism.

Although this is part of a larger problem which will be covered later it is possible to see if there are feasible alternative systems. One of course is a total change in the management of society towards central control; another is compulsory lodging of centralised information. The first sounds unattractive and is unattractive; the second, although it could lead to central control need not do so given the right circumstances. For example, the 1975 Industry Act enacts the concept of planning Agreements and within those Agreements investment and manpower Planning decisions will be laid down. It would be possible specifically to note those changes which are thought to be due to computers and let the Manpower Services Commission know. Each individual decision is taken without knowledge of other decisions which may actually have affected the original decision. We have, in other words, to invest or plan on imperfect information. It must be in everyone's interests to improve that information. The alternative method of course is to insist that computer installations are reported to the Manpower Services Commission well in advance of their operative state and discussions take place on the likely manpower release and training implications. It is feasible, and it is highly desirable.

The Swedish Labour Market mechanisms seem able to accomplish this. Manpower changes are not confined to the redundancy situation. There are many instances where the computer has created jobs; indeed, created a company or industry. Obviously the computer manufacturing industry is one, and the peripheral manufacturing another, while the agencies, consultancies and bureaux must, be definition, owe their existence to the computer. There are, however, other instances of increasing employment. We have mentioned the increase in clerical staffs often needed with an installation, not only in the operators to managers range but also in the data-preparation staff. the 'manual' staff, and the staff employed to collate the information as a standardised product. Then there are the industries that have been created. It is almost impossible to envisage the rapid growth and immense penetration of the credit-card system if computers had not been available to process all the debits and this industry now employs an increasingly large number of people. The same applies to the Post Office Giro, which could not function without computers.

Job creation, like redundancy, can create many problems, though they are basically very different ones. If jobs are created in any one area, unless there is a pool of trained labour in that area there will be bottlenecks, unskilled staff used, or a bidding away of other enterprises' staffs. It is thus just as necessary to notify the Manpower Services Commission that job vacancies will arise, well in advance of the time when they actually become available so that all the necessary training, retraining and mobility problems can be undertaken and overcome. The situation is by no means confined to the computer, yet as a tool the effects of the computer are so much more far-reaching and extravagant than others that such labour-force changes should be monitored and controlled before all other problems.

Trade unions have always reacted sharply to technological redundancies and the print unions' long fight against newspaper production's automation is but an example of this. Sooner or later, however, technology triumphs and this in the course of human history is not surprising, but that triumph must not be at the expense of ordinary employees. The present *ad hoc* system of job placements will not help the unemployed printers, and their redundancy pay will prove to be less of a nest-egg and more a rapidly depleting supplement to transfer payments. Unions cannot stand in the way of technological progress, but nor can they stand by and watch their members being sacrificed in its name. If increasingly violent confrontations are to be avoided then mechanisms such as those sketched out above must be computed and found, not just for the short term, but certainly for longer-term industrial and social harmony.

Chapter 10

Unions use computers too

Unions are now considered to be fair game for computer salesmen if the numbers of prospective sellers and providers visiting unions with glowing reports of their wares are any indication of the whole trend. It is hardly surprising. Trade unions, or at least, the largest of them, are now huge concerns with large cash flows, large salary bills to meet and considerable administrative problems. There are 106 TUC affiliated trade unions with a total membership of over 10 million, yet the distribution of members is skewed very markedly. The largest ten unions have between them 6,956,000 members and the range is from 1.8 million to nineteen, a rather considerable difference. Quite obviously, the smaller the union the less likely it is either to want, or need or, indeed, be able to afford the services of a computer so the salesmen have a rather narrowed-down field in which to operate. Perhaps that is why they are trying so hard.

The TUC held a computer-use conference in January 1972 but has since done little about the subject, although in truth, trade unions differ so much that the exercise had very limited practical value. At that time twelve unions had either purchased, hired or leased a computer or used bureaux services, but no survey has been done since then and as unions are most jealous regarding information about membership and organisation such information is difficult to get. This makes a further survey more difficult but it is believed that now over twenty unions use computer services, the increase being mainly accounted for by increased bureaux use rather than purchase or leasing.

No two trade unions have identical administrative systems, rather the differences are most marked, yet it is in this area that the movement makes most use of computers.

Rather like private companies and other agencies, the trade union has administrative bottlenecks, has to pay salaries and in short, has to have an efficient cost-minimising day-to-day existence. Unlike, however, these other organisations a trade union is a democratic body which is answerable to a membership and as we shall see this can become a constraint to full utilisation of a computer's capabilities.

Unions consist of members. Each member pays a subscription. While these are two basic features of bona fide trade unions are held in common, very little else is. To understand how unions do use, and perhaps will use computers it is first preferable to draw up a model of some non-existent union, how it is organised and what are its needs.

Members have to be grouped into administrative units, both for the purpose of records and meetings and, perhaps, for negotiating purposes. Let us call this unit 'Branch' and let us assume that it never has less than 200 members but is unlikely to have more than 1,000. ASTMS has 800 Branches while a union the size of the Engineering Workers has nearer 3,000. Branches will be aggregated on a geographical basis to form Divisions or Districts or Regions or, perhaps, both Regions and Divisions. There will be, perhaps, twenty Divisions and between four and six Regions in a union with over 200,000 members. The first thing a union must do is collect its subscriptions and keep records of them. Here we have to leave the model and explore briefly the different systems.

The Branch has traditionally been the collecting agency. Each Branch will have elected officials, generally unpaid, and may elect collectors, although in some instances the treasurer may fulfil this function. Subscriptions may be collected by hand in cash or cheque form, may be paid by bankers' order or draft to the Branch or may be deducted directly from the member's salary by the employer. In the last instance the subscription is then forwarded either to the Branch or to the union's head office, and is called 'check-off'. In some such cases the employer makes a charge on a percentage basis for the trouble caused and work done. The subscriptions themselves vary between unions both in amount and in type. Most unions have more than one subscription rate, say, less for young people or to allow pensioners the right to retain union membership but some have far more complicated systems than others.

At one end is the basic single rate for all non-retired members while at the other is a fixed percentage of basic salary up to a cut-off point. In between these are contributions fixed with different rates for different salary bands, age-related contributions up to probably 21, contribution rates dependent upon status bands or a system of levies based on a percentage of negotiated wage increases. Whatever the system, a computer can cope easily enough, although the more subscription rates there are, the more difficult it becomes to handle manually. The monies basically get channelled to the union head office but generally the Branch takes a fixed percentage and so does the Division and Region so that the union can run locally without contacting headquarters for small amounts of cash while in addition Branch officials, all or some, may receive some form of honorarium.

The inflow of money enables the union to run but its collection has functions beyond this as we shall see. Branches keep records of members and are charged with 'lapsing' members who get too far behind with their subscriptions (generally from 3 to 6 months), and will submit returns to head office at monthly, quarterly and/or half-yearly intervals. These returns will indicate membership, areas of contributions, etc. When monies and returns reach head office they are filed, checked and placed in the appropriate fund. Again, the type and number of funds will differ from union to union. For example, some have Friendly Society types of benefit, some have political levy monies and some have specific dispute-funds.

Obviously, a large union with many Branches, different subscription rates and many separate funds will have to employ a large number of clerical staff if computers are not used to process subscriptions. It would therefore seem to be a cut and dried case, computer time equals more efficiency, therefore use a computer. Add to this the fact that local Branch officials are often in full-time employment, with the union work to be done in their spare time, unpaid, and that because of the work-load it is difficult to get volunteers let alone anyone willing to contest elections and the case for the union use of computers becomes even stronger, at least in this field of administration.

Unions, however, are not quite like other organisations. They are irrevocably based on democratic elections, whether of lay members or paid officials. The computer, as we have seen, has the tendency to stimulate centralisation and in practice this may well run counter to a basic union ethos. In more detail this can be seen quite clearly.

The Branch is the primary contact between members and the union structure. If subscriptions were paid directly to head office the contact between collectors and members would be lost or the stimulus to attend Branch meetings to pay 'subs' would be lost (and so would the contact and debate). Whichever is true the link between the member and the union has been weakened. This is most important, especially at a time when the media and, indeed, unions themselves, are worried about the lack of attendance at meetings with the resulting lack of participation having consequences on both political and industrial levels. It is possible to have a system where payments are made directly to the Branch and these are then forwarded directly to head office who keep the money, arrange for the percentage deductions to be returned to the Branches and Divisions and make up accounts, arrears and membership audits for the Branches at regular intervals. This method would, if checks are to be made, involve a duplication of records at Branch and head-office levels which could be avoided by using computers.

A compromise method may be to use an on-line system with terminals in each Divisional office. Subscriptions would be paid into the Branches which would then automatically forward them to the Divisional office and from there they could be directed straight into a central data-bank, and immediate Branch accounts returned along the same route. As well as subscriptions, membership records and records of members out of compliance (not paid up) must be maintained. This is a relatively easy task if a program has already been written for subscription collection as it reflects the subscription flows. There is generally a large turnover of members in the larger unions, new employees join while others leave their jobs and move totally out of the union's sphere of influence, fail to pay subscriptions, or die. This turnover is superimposed on the change of address, a phenomenon which NALGO, for example, estimate affects 30 per cent of their membership every year. Again, the changes in membership and the turnover of addresses argue strongly for a computerised records section providing that adequate information is made available. It is, however, essential that the local Branches, Divisions or Regions know their membership and have their own lists if they are not to lose autonomy and authority.

Unions with their own installation use them for these purposes. The AUEW, the EETPU and TASS all check contributions, make up Branch accounts, check their membership and monitor check-offs and have a national numbering system. Unions who use bureaux tend not to use them for these purposes but for payrolling, etc., although at least two do and ASTMS did try some years ago to extend this service. In two union cases the programs used were far too simplistic to cope with the complexities of union administration and the union's method of data collection was not changed sufficiently to provide adequate imputs into the computer. The situation in one got so bad after 12 months and considerable cost that the scheme was abandoned, more records department staff had to be hired and it took two-and-a-half years to get the records and Branch finances back into a workable state. The computer, however, can solve many administrative problems (for example, the time-consuming analysis and keeping of records and the automatic printing of envelopes) and in this respect some unions have been more fortunate than the Civil Service Union which stated in 1972 'The data produced by the computer has been so prone to error as to render it practically useless.'

National data is, as we suggested in an earlier chapter, not generally of very great use to a union; it represents the icing while members are concerned with the cake and the odd sultana. There are, however, good reasons for having a national register and a national numbering system. The larger unions use one or more journals or other forms of written communication and although in many instances these are delivered in bulk to the place of work, some unions send them directly to the member's home. This obviously needs an up-to-date address system and equally obviously requires pre-printed wrappers to be provided to the printers for speedy distribution – a union with hundreds of thousands of members could not cope with this without computer aids. If communication is vital, then regular weekly mailings from head office to Branches are also important and again, with large unions, computer aid is of help with addressing and mailing but given the far smaller number of Branches than members, it is hardly indispensible for this purpose. The other use to which a national list can be put is balloting for elections and this requires some explanation.

Postal balloting in the trade-union movement has become a party political issue to the extent that a TV political broadcast on behalf of the Conservative Party was devoted to the subject and supported postal balloting together with detailed Press orchestration. The traditional method of voting has always been on a Branch basis with attendance at Branch meetings as prerequisite for voting. As attendances at Branch meetings is historically low the argument is that those elected in this manner are not representative of the membership as a whole. This argument is made by hostile commentators and is intended to disguise the real objective which is to get a leadership that most fits in with their prejudices. Although this would not be the inevitable result of postal ballots, it is premised on the fact that those who bother to attend the one voting Branch meeting per year, or even per 5 years, are more interested in both politics and industrial relations and would therefore be more 'militant'. It is argued that postal balloting would allow those who never attend Branch meetings to vote and thus get a better representation!

If national elections by postal ballot are to be run secretly and efficiently the ballot paper will have to be sent to the members' home addresses rather than the work-place where holidays, sickness and employers' internal post systems all come into the reckoning. For this a union must be able to rely on addresses and numbers, and a computer is by far the best, fastest and most reliable method. It could also be programmed to count the vote! To attempt postal voting without a computer or without an outside agency's aid could well be disastrous for the average middle-sized union with the clerical work involved and an average membership mobility.

Computers can thus help in the administration of cash flows, distribution of literature and communications and the running of elections. Two of the three (distribution of literature being the exception) can have grave repercussions on the democratic framework of trade unions and because of this the unions have shown a reserve in using computer facilities and have remained unconvinced, by the weight of salesmanship to which they have been subjected.

However, these are not the only functions to which computer hire can be put and nor are these the only constraints to its use. As with any other concern, computers can be, and are, used to service the payroll, adjust for taxation and National Insurance contributions for employees in the trade-union movement. As the range of services offered by unions increases, so the number of staff they employ increases, throwing a heavier administrative burden on the wages staff, and a bureaux service, with a pre-packaged program, is both easier and relatively inexpensive. But again, unions differ somewhat from the normal commercial or Government situation.

Some unions have their own pension schemes, not for the staff, but for members, and in cases where unions use computers they administer them through the normal data-processing channels and the same is done for any Friendly Society benefits that may be offered. For the most part these sort of benefits are part of the smaller and older craft-union packages and these are precisely the organisations which do not use computers. Contribution cards can be issued by computer, cheques can be written and invoices and bills entered up and paid, in short, a full range of services can be and is provided by computers to a limited number of trade unions.

Other and more specifically trade-union oriented tasks can also be undertaken. The AUEW has a data-bank of agreements analysed under 260 different factors and in theory provides a 24 hour retrieval service for members. Although we have looked at this research function earlier and suggested that the approximations that need to be made may make the resulting data unreliable, it is significant that at least one union has decided to use its spare computer capacity for this purpose. It would also be possible to monitor disputes and automatically pay dispute-pay using a data-bank and a simple program, while other functions could include the slightly more complex educational package for use in the training school program. Matters such as maintenance accounting for property owned by the union and budget projections as well as daily or weekly reports to senior officials are all possible and are either being done or being contemplated by trade unions with computer installations.

Probably the major thing about computer-use lies in the fact that some of the major unions have not installed one but simply use bureaux in the strictly managerial areas of wages, pension deductions, etc. The General and Municipal Workers Union, the third largest union does not possess an installation, nor do several of the other 'big ten'.

Other organisations of the size of these unions, which together, have 2 million members, would certainly use computers and one must explore the reasons for their choice if any sense is to be made of smaller unions using them more fully.

Before getting an installation or deciding to go to a bureaux any prospective user has to ask what the costs and the benefits will be? In a Government or commercial sphere the aim is to increase efficiency, undertake new work and research and maximise profits. In the trade-union movement the aim must be to increase efficiency and cut costs. The question then becomes 'will an installation of the size needed to generate the requisite power be so expensive as to overweigh any savings made and at what cost is increased efficiency achieved?' Both the AUEW and the EETPU use large ICL machines (1920s) and employ a considerable number of data-processing staff; eighteen at the EETPU and over thirty at the AUEW. This staffing problem can itself lead to anomalies, as in the case of one union where the computer manager was being paid the market rate on salary that was considerably higher than the General Secretary's. Although to date there have been no redundancy problems reported by unions after switching to computer use, it must also be claimed that there has been no increase in staff either so let us assume that the labour cost effect is neutral. There are also the running costs, capital costs, service costs, materials and building charges to meet, while against these are savings in stationery and Branch officials' time. The difference between these two is the money cost of increased efficiency. However, there are other costs too. It has been estimated that to use a computer to its optimum there needs to be 2½ million members. The AUEW only use their computer for 8 hours per day because they feel that at present the marginal costs involved in setting up a night shift would not be matched by productivity gains. The EETPU on the other hand use their spare capacity by acting as a bureaux for two other unions and have formed a joint organisation run between themselves and an employers' organisation.

Neither the GMWU nor, indeed, the other top ten unions, such as NUPE, ASTMS, and USDAW, have seen the efficiency advantages outweighing the costs. The growth of mini-computers and silicon chips, which may give as much power and storage capacity as the larger machines while costing many times less and needing fewer trained staff, may reverse their attitudes. There is still, however, the resistance built up by others' experiences of computerisation. There is also this nagging doubt as to whether the democratic processes could be irredeemably damaged.

A major reason advanced for computerisation is that it is impossible to get an adequate number of Branch officials and that it is thus incumbent on the central apparatus to take over their role. Although it is true that Branch officials are often overworked and are difficult to attract, centralisation could ultimately kill the Branch system by removing its basic union functions. Negotiations are generally carried out either nationally or by separate groups within a Branch, the Branch being the social and political arm of the union. If the Branch system wilts so the chances of alienation of the rank-and-file membership will increase. Not only will the employer be remote, not only will the Government be remote but the trade union will be remote too and at the lowest but most important levels of the organisation the individual member will be dwarfed by institutions over which he has no control at all. The considerations are then on two levels; monetary and fundamental social organisation.

As has been said an on-line Divisional office system is probably the answer but such systems are not only expensive but need trained personnel in the peripheral offices. The other answer is for unions to use installations in a more realistic way by utilising their full potential for research and analysis. It has been suggested by some that a standard program can be written for wage claims but this is unrealistic, given the different types of claim that a general union undertakes each year. There is no doubt that wage claims may be helped by computer-use and that industry or company studies can be undertaken on a far more technical and informed basis. Fundamentally what has to be decided is whether a union needs a computer or not and if so what sort of access it needs.

If payrolling, etc., is the only need then a bureaux is the cheapest and most efficient form of use. If, on the other hand, it is decided to take the other administrative tasks on board, then what has to be decided is whether a computer will be optimally used. Certainly the mini-computer has simplified the choices but it is still possible to have a shares installation among a consortium of unions using the time available in the most efficient manner. As unions merge, and there is a growing list of them, so the units become larger and the need for computers becomes more apparent. It is reasonable to project that by 1984 there will be less than fifty effective unions of which at least forty will have their own installation of some description. Communication, education, finance, records, disputes, planning, planning agreements and economic models will all be part and parcel of a future trade union's data-bank. What the unions' members will have to do is to safeguard themselves against centralised decision-making based on computer output and ensure their own rights in what are basically the only extra-governmental democratic institutions in Britain. If the computer destroys this democracy it will have done a great disservice to both sides of industry – care must be taken and thought given to the future. A 1960s-type rush will have more far-reaching effects than a massive slump to follow, if these are only reflected in the increased number of unofficial disputes following the breakdown of communications and effective control procedures.

Chapter 11

Checks and balances

The computer affects techniques of co-existence as well. It has become an essential tool for both the mechanics and the administration of most large businesses and the Government. Within these enterprises some of the subjects themselves could not be properly handled without the computer. We have already looked at the role of the computer for the remuneration package and how this newish concept would probably not exist without it. There are, however, other factors which affect the relationship between the employees and management of an enterprise which do not, strictly speaking, come into the realms of that package but which nevertheless either depend on their existence or for their effectiveness on the computer.

Modern society has evolved a complex industrial, commercial and governmental structure, all inter-related. In response to this a plethora of conditions, national linkages, safeguards, checks and balances, evaluations and structures have been brought into being. Some affect a work-force in the collective sense, others affect the majority, while yet others affect their personal lives. These areas are growing in importance in relation to the running of enterprises and are increasingly coming into the orbit of trade unions, but several of the matters are so technical as to demand both sophistication and expertise from the members and officials. If the unions' representation of their members is to develop and be complete training of those responsible for dealing with these matters must be undertaken.

One of the growth areas in British management techniques has been that of productivity and productivity bargaining – only disrupted by Government incomes policies. Payment by results has been a favourite form of remuneration for literally centuries. From feudal days when payment was a percentage of the crops grown and thus the more grown, the more retained, through the craft guild to the industrial revolution with its piecework in the mills, mines and factories, productivity payments have been well used. For most of this period they acted fairly and squarely against the interests of employees. In some cases there were no payments outside piecework – no output equalled no pay, even though the lack of output was due to factors totally beyond the control of the work-force. Mine disasters, harvest failures, failure of suppliers to deliver, all rebounded more on the employees than the owners. Within Britain today there are still industries where piecework-rates earnings represent by far the greatest component of remuneration; the construction industry is one notorious example and there are many more where salesmen's commissions and bonuses play a major part.

Government policy, however, has been the main stimulus to the growth of productivity bargaining. The emphasis has changed from a company's desire to minimise the costs (and optimise its profits) to macro-economic policy considerations; that is from the consideration of the small unit to the overview of the needs of the economy as a whole. Successive Governments have realised that one of the major problems in Britain has been low productivity when compared with industry in competing countries and have felt it desirable that policies should be pursued which increased output. One method seized upon was to encourage productivity bargaining in a time of general wage restraint policy. The Labour Government did this in 1968 and its Acts to a great extent acted as the genesis of the current system. In passing it is worth noting that we are talking about labour productivity as opposed to returns on capital equipment, a distinction not precisely made by Government and often not sufficiently understood. Many industrial disputes have taken place because output per employee has increased and the employer has insisted that this has been exclusively the result of the installation of new capital equipment. The argument has certainly not been resolved in principle, and one suspects that until such a time as a rational approach is worked out, productivity bargaining will develop inbuilt frustrations.

When, in the 'good old days', a company produced one product and was proud of it, productivity was an easy concept to grasp. It was a matter of counting the number of widgets or whatever, produced by an individual, although a new widget-making machine could have upset the balance. Those days, however, are long gone. British industry is dominated by the multi-plant and multi-product company, some of which are also multinational. There is intra-group trading at transfer prices; there are production processes in which employees play only a small part in the output of the final product and there are employees – and a growing number of them – who have no physical product as a final output allocatable to them. This is where the computer enters on to the scene. Production processes can be broken down into their various individual components, and individual employees identified with each component of output. To do this without a computer is a very heavy administrative burden, but it can easily be done using computers and the relevant information techniques. This is not, however, the only method for calculating productivity payments, nor is it the only use of the computer in the payment of productivity earnings.

The productivity scheme may not be based on individual performance. In the context of a production-line process it is most unlikely that any individual employee can produce more of his or her output than any other member of the line, purely because the track moves at the same speed for all and the number of components moving along the track is the same for all. In such cases piecework is determined for the whole group of workers, although the rate of remuneration may vary from job to job on the same line, depending on skill, basic salary, etc. Alternatively there may be a scheme which works out the productivity in company terms and divides the resultant payment equally or differentially on a predetermined basis between all employees. In all of these cases the output plus the people actually working in its production has to be recorded and a calculation made as to which employee gets what return at the end of the week, month, or year. These calculations can be very complex. The part that groups of workers play in production, the number of hours worked, the payment function, all have to be calculated and if an enterprise employs 10,000 people this must either entail the use of computers or a very large number of clerical staff if payment is to be made in any reasonable time.

After the Labour Government stimulated the idea of productivity bargaining it not unnaturally spread to the white-collar sector, otherwise white-collar staffs would have been left behind as far as remuneration was concerned. Typists have worked on an output related bonus system for many years, but the average clerical employee does not have a very measurable output. An insurance or shipping clerk, for example, can measure the number of documents passing through his or her hands each day, or the value of a life policy, but that is about all; for that matter how does a data-processing worker measure productivity – by output? As a result complicated systems of productivity schemes have been initiated which leaned heavily on computer use. Basically they rely upon the idea that a given number of employees can do a particular amount of work in a specified time-scale. This work varies by department and naturally as departments are inter-related each individual output will depend upon the other's performance and thus the calculations start to become complicated. Each department may handle different forms, etc., from other departments and from and to external sources so that the number of combinations can spiral. Schedules are produced and, at the end of the year, a formula based on the excess of services handled per head of staff over and above the norm laid down is put into money terms and paid as a productivity bonus. In essence this type of scheme relies upon two factors, one of which is the level of staffing and the other the level of general business. The level of business is totally out of the hands of ordinary workers and assuming a constant level productivity increases can only be achieved by staff reductions.

The type of scheme must involve the use of a computer, a use which is a general extension of its normal functions of invoicing, billing and recording. When a standard is set, the union has to agree to it and to do so must understand both the calculation itself and the method by which it was reached. This needs an expertise in quasi-accountancy and computer jargon because the last thing a management will do is to translate 'print-outs' into comprehensible English for the benefit of trade unions, although the Employee Protection Act provisions for the divulging of information will help in the future. Trade-union officials, or at least the specialist departments such as research within trade unions, are thus having to cope with computer technology and the interpretation of jargon with documentation which, a decade ago, would have been thought impossible.

Bonus schemes, based on increased profitability and employee participation in that profit, as paid to employees in stockbrokers offices and the commission paid to sales representatives, are again well established by custom. However, as the concern increases in size and the number of relevant employees increases so does the need for accurate records, especially when dealing with a non-physical product such as insurance; the obvious solution is to use a computer. In such cases if the bonus is challenged, and this might well happen if a union wishes to renegotiate the rate of payment and is looking at the global sums paid over a year, the union official will have to cope with the breakdown of calculations and this again requires some degree of expertise.

The major problem is still, however, the degree to which new capital equipment adds, or perhaps subtracts from labour productivity. The computer has a different role to play in many of these arguments. We mentioned in an earlier chapter the troubles that can arise when production line speeds are raised or lowered generally after a computer analysis or perhaps actually controlled by the computer. This can lead to either the employer trying to reduce the rate at which piecework is paid or attempting to drop the system entirely and move on to what is known as 'measured day work'. This is done on the grounds that the existing payment system would result in the company having to provide total earnings in excess of the amount they think suitable. Translated into the cold light of collective bargaining it means all the productivity gains are kept by the company and the employee is working harder for the same remuneration – not something that union members tend to welcome. In other cases, automated equipment and computer-controlled processes have gone hand in hand with a reduction in staff with the concomitant total increase in productivity and a larger increase in productivity per employee. When the electrical power engineers took industrial action in 1972 it was basically because this situation had occurred against them. The employers refused to acknowledge that any of the productivity increase was due to employees working harder and insisted it was all due to the extra capital employed. Although this was settled after a dislocating action it is in an area where the issue will undoubtedly raise its head again as new and better equipment becomes operational.

Productivity bargaining is, however, far from being the only fringe area where computers and unions meet. Another important one is the checking of information. If there is computerised record keeping, or if a computerised productive process is in operation, details of performance, aggregates, and averages for individuals, are obtainable very quickly, whereas in the past such data was dependent upon a long time lapse probably coinciding with traditional audit and stock-taking times. The productivity scheme based on excess output or traffic over a predetermined norm depends on this use of the computer, but it is not only in formal schemes that union members are affected. If no scheme exists the situation of the union member is somewhat worse, his possibility of reward is correspondingly diminished, but the chances of penalisation are correspondingly increased.

Comparisons of individual or group performance against the whole have traditionally lain with the company and unless some arrangement has been made the employees will not have access to the data. This means that management attitudes to employees are determined by information to which those employees have no access and thus often no method of knowing why they are being stayed, ignored or promoted. It is one matter to have a continuous assessment programme where there is a countersigning provision by the employee and an appeal system; it is quite another where the assessment is made covertly. Many companies have been moved to introduce merit payments on top of basic salary either as a method of moving through a salary range or on a more *ad hoc* and opportunistic basis. These payments are generally undesirable from the point of view of trade unions. Whereas bank staffs have published merit scales, the overwhelming majority remain secret and are never published. This means that a management can pay a bonus of, let us say, £200 per annum and claim (to the individual) that this is very high, while it may be the lowest in the whole department. The effect is firstly to reduce total payments, with one person being played off against another and the secrecy allowing for neither group pressure nor adequate comparators for individual pressure and secondly to place each employee at a disadvantage and in a position of undue dependency.

From a trade union point of view this is unacceptable. The premisses on which the comparisons are made are not known and have therefore to be taken on total trust. Computers as machines can make mistakes because of human errors and make them more repetitively and quickly than other machines. Thus remuneration on the one hand and disciplinary procedures or promotion prospects on the other hand are dependent on a machine totally within the control of management alone and employees, or their representative unions, have so far had no method of interposing themselves into the system.

Interestingly, it is in the junior and middle management ranks where this system strikes the hardest, although the role of the computer may differ slightly. Managers have control functions as well as being responsible for their individual element of output and this control can range from financial to man-management. Records easily retrieved by the computer on a given program can highlight all sorts of anomalies or set standards by which managerial staffs can be judged. For example, the strike record of the employees under one manager may be considerably different from the normal pattern, or the financial control less stringent in that costs on non-essentials have escalated over the budgeted amount. Although such details are useful in monitoring the progress of a department there is no balancing system of appeal and a manager's career could be blighted merely because of a series of accidents which cannot show up on the computer print-out, or indeed be built into the program to influence the print-out.

In all these cases it is not the fact that the mechanism exists that is disquieting to unions. It is the lack of employee participation and the secrecy that are worrying and this is compounded by the use of the computer. Separate systems do not have to be set up; these need only to be a new program to get out new information and the employee has no idea that the check is being made. It is rather like having a secret TV camera somewhere looking at you, you do not know whether it is ever switched on, let alone what it is looking for. Before the advent of the computer such checks would have involved many people, and would have needed interviews with those being checked, interviews where, if requested and if practicable, a union official could have accompanied the employee. Now, however, this chance of pre-empting misunderstanding and inequities is disappearing and if the union is involved it will be after the check and thus, yet again, the employee is placed in a defensive, reactive position.

Many employers insist on medical examinations before an offer of employment is made and then check-ups at various intervals through a working lifetime. The rationale behind this insistance varies but will include the reasonable desire of an employer to minimise the sick pay and maximise the work done or may spring from a sense of paternal welfare. In other instances it may be that the productive process entails some health hazard and yet another cause may be that the insurance company administering the pension scheme insists on protecting its investments with a health check. Whatever the reason, medicals are now a regular feature of employees' lives. Records have to be kept of these examinations and they usually find themselves in a computer data-bank.

The question of the confidentiality of the information then arises. Who is entitled to look at, discuss and evaluate employees' health records? This is important not merely in the case of a person who has had some unsociable disease and wishes, not unnaturally, to restrict the dissemination of such information, but it may impinge on work and promotion prospects or even the ability to get a new job. When health records are kept in an ordinary filing system it is usually done under lock and key; the problem with the computer is that it is easy for a trained person to obtain the information without either attracting suspicion or leaving any trace of the deed. The other problem, minor though it may sound, is the accuracy of retrieval. One feature of company medicals is that frequently the employee is not told the result and when a mistake occurs, for example, because there are two different men with the same surname and initials, neither man is in a sure position to say the record is wrong. The usual computer horror stories on this subject abound but it should be made clear that this is still a rare occurrence in a well-run and well-programmed installation.

Another growing feature of corporate life is job evaluation. Consultancies which specialise in this form of practise are fond of saying that although you cannot compare apples with oranges, you can rank them in a logical order. Obviously so difficult a task, and one which nature is so ill-equipped to cope with, must need a computer somewhere in its operation. Although many misconceptions abound in an employer's approach to job evaluation, in objective terms the process is to get a ranking order acceptable to most of the employees, which is logical and upon which a salary system can be superimposed. Although it is generally the large employers, both private and public, who employ this technique, small employers are not precluded from using it, although the close relationships among a more tightly knit staff make it more difficult to operate in practice. There are many forms of job evaluation and many consultancies to market them.

In essence, all rely on a points system, whether overt or hidden. For example, the system might identify several factors, each of which is present in jobs in the organisation to some extent; these might be experience, accountability, decision-making, etc., or might include health hazards, tedium or, indeed, any factor one can think of. Points are then awarded for the degree to which the job reflects each particular characteristic, perhaps on a scale from 1 to 10. Each factor is then weighed against the others so that the total comes to 1 or 100 or any constant number. The points are added up and a ranking system established. It sounds easy and perhaps is easy. Unfortunately, the system depends almost totally on the weightings given to the factors and the choice of the factors themselves. It is not, for instance, very difficult to imagine a situation where the majority of employees are women and a highly rated factor is physical strength, thus perpetuating discrimination.

But this is only part of a larger problem. There is probably no single technique which has engendered so much passion and produced so much dissatisfaction as job evaluation, especially in the white-collar sectors. No one likes to be told that their job is less important than another person's, especially when previously the job had appeared to be rated equally, so, not surprisingly, employees treat job evaluation with a fair degree of suspicion. In a town dominated by one employer we are aware that wives had accepted that their husbands were stock controllers or traffic managers with discrete salaries but when they were all job evaluated and tagged by numbers and letters there were grave fissions of discontent and dissatisfaction within the community which fed back into the firm's appeal machinery. Trade unions are now always consulted by their members in cases where a job evaluation is mooted and the union has several functions to perform. The first is to approve or at least tolerate to the degree of cooperating with, the consultancy concerned. The other functions are more technical.

Because the final result depends on the selection and then the weightings of the factors to be used, the union has to check these, not in the abstract but in the circumstances peculiar to the organisation. Job descriptions will be detailed and again will need to be checked and finally the finished calculations cannot just be taken on trust. One technique which leans on the computer is the 'consensus method'. Here, in theory at least, the factors and the weightings are ultimately determined by employees themselves after having sample job descriptions. To make calculations easier a standard program is used. The final print-out must be checked thoroughly, if for no other reason than to see whether easily avoidable anomolous positions have arisen. The whole exercise requires that union members have a knowledge of the philosophy underlining the analysis and the ability to question the professional evaluators, including the programming and the assumptions on which it is based. As a final point, unions always insist on an appeal mechanism so that aggrieved employees can have an opportunity to change the decision (although it must be recognised that it is the job and not the employee that is being evaluated).

In almost all instances there are many such appeals and usually a generous proportion of successful ones in the first instance. It does argue that job evaluation, for all its quasi-scientific jargon and computer use, is still art-form and to be approached with caution.

In the United States, employers have taken their personnel and interviewing functions more seriously than in Britain. A wife being subjected to interview before her husband can get a job or be promoted is a commonplace across the Atlantic but a little-used technique in Britain. Indeed, the Sex-Discrimination Act may happily outlaw it. Psychological motivation testing or ink-dot identification is used as well as more subtle but rather insidious interview methods. Of these, one at least makes use of the computer.

The applicant sits in a room with four or more interviewers. He or she is asked questions which one would reasonably expect to be put, about experience, the job, probing capabilities and direct attitudes. Mixed in with this line of questioning are, however, other questions, some, apparently, incorrectly chosen and suggesting to the applicant that the interviewer is mad while other questions asked conceivably just fit into a normal interview pattern. The answers to these questions are then fed into a prepared computer program designed to evaluate the morals, trustworthiness, obedience and mental attitudes of the applicant. Although this sounds reasonable, consider the problems of programming such a package. It presupposes that answers will be in a certain range, anything outside this range, however subtle, correct or perhaps wrong, must be treated as though no answer was given. Consider a case beautifully handled in a recent German film 'Kaspar Hauser'. Kaspar is asked the usual riddle of finding out which of two men always tells the truth when the other always tells lies. Instead of the normal answer Kaspar says he would ask one of them 'whether he was a tree-frog'. This subtle and correct method was far outside the range of answers that the interrogator would accept and would undoubtedly be far outside the range of any computer program. The types of questions asked are those which could well elicit such a clever response yet in programming terms the answer must be wrong.

Trade unions have traditionally had little influence and have sought little influence over interviewing procedures. The type of interview described above does, however, have indirect implications for employees. It is mainly the middle or senior management personnel who are subjected to this procedure and the result must be to hire not only risk-avoiders but also those who conform to traditional patterns. In other words, the unconventional mind could not survive such a test although a major shortcoming in British industry has been the lack of flair in management; a lack which has contributed to the progressive decline in our industrial base. Such interview techniques can only reinforce this decline and thus place even more jobs in jeopardy.

Some posts carry a good deal of financial responsibility, not in the sense of being responsible for millions of pounds of investment decisions, but the carrying of cash or the handling of cheques. Insurance salesmen, some bank and security company employees, clerks and sales staff all have a chance to 'Make off with the goodies'. A few employers find that they cannot get insurance companies to insure them against theft unless such staff are 'fidelity-bonded'. Fidelity bonding is carried out by specialist companies who, in the course of their business, have to carry out extensive personal and financial checks on employees. Credit worthiness, including late payments, propensity to drink or gamble, criminal record or liability for maintenance payments are among the things that a bonding company will investigate.

Such intensive scrutiny will almost certainly involve the use of data-banks, either legally or extra-legally and it is here that troubles can and have started. Mistakes, as we have seen and all know, do occur; the wrong name is used, incorrect data has been fed in to the computer, the program may be faulty. Whatever the reason, there is a real chance that incorrect data is used either to accept or reject a person for a 'fidelity bond'. As it is the bonding company which stands to lose the money if a bonding is made in error, such companies tend to lean on to the side of harshness in their judgements – in other words, refuse bondings.

Consider the following case of a man who was appointed to a senior insurance salesman job with a brokerage. His appointment was conditional upon a bond but after 3 months the bonding company informed his new employer that he was not trustworthy and they would not indemnify him. The brokerage had no alternative but to fire the man though they considered him honest and a good employee. His union raised the matter but neither the bonding company nor the brokerage would divulge the reason for the withholding of the bond. Finally, after much pressure it was established that it was withheld because of the late payment of a hire-purchase instalment. This in itself seems a slight reason. What makes matters worse is that the man in question had paid off all the sum outstanding some 4 months earlier and not only was he not late, he was a zealous payer. The computer had not recorded this payment in the same section as instalment credits and debits.

Now consider the man. He was not only out of a job but he was also branded as a person who could not be bonded and his chances of similar employment are precisely zero. The bonding company refused to change its opinion on the grounds that the information it received was accurate, which, in semantic terms it was. It was the computer print-out that was wrong. This man is now unemployed and unemployable and is suing (with the union's legal assistance) the bonding company and the original hire purchase company, with, it must be added, little success.

It is dangerous to argue from the particular to the general and so it is unwise to condemn all bonding on one case. In broader terms, however, it raises two fundamental points. The first is the lack of privacy surrounding the original hire-purchase transaction and the second the complete inflexibility of computer-based information. It becomes yet another piece of evidence in favour of controls, checks and balances.

Some employers have, for many years, employed a 'black-list'. This dates from the early days of trade unionism and was intended to ensure that union activists would not be able to pursue their craft or trade. Obviously in the early days the communication's limitations meant that 'black listing' was confined to one geographical area and limited to companies which knew each other, although given the lack of mobility among the work-force this was adequate enough.

As employers' federations grew, and as telephonic, telex and other communications improved so central filing and immediate central checking became possible. The computer has now made the black-list a much more viable entity. Names can be sent from an employer to a central data-bank and retrieval can be made in a matter of minutes. There is no appeal against such a listing by an employee because the lists do not officially exist; wrong names can be entered and totally unsuspecting people deprived of a job. The black-list procedure is still prevalent, especially in the construction industry. An adjunct of this system is the Civil Service type listing where certain employees and union officials are not allowed to represent their members on security sensitive sites. Neither of these techniques are new but both depend for their effectiveness in a modern age on computer use.

In all of this interface (a computer word for which 'meeting' is a far more acceptable substitute) between the computer and the union there lies the need to know about the technical procedures. It is only too easy to accept computer data as inevitably correct and to lie back and receive the result. Union officials and members are learning to question the underlying premisses on which decisions are based and to realise and then adjust to the limitations of computer analysis. Having mastered this the officials will then have to acquire the expertise to monitor the implementation of decisions. An example not covered in this chapter may show the inherent dangers. Operations analysis often forms part of a corporate-planning department and unions, through Planning Agreements, are being drawn more into this side of industrial life. The union member or official in a car company will have to accept the corporate prediction of the demand for its cars and thus employment prospects, unless he or she can get behind the data to see what variables have been used in the computer model. The company may, for example, intend closing the plant and use imports from one of its foreign subsidiaries to fill the gap which currently is not an outlandish suggestion.

Without both a computer appreciation course and a basic knowledge of business techniques, such a check is impossible. The unionist does not need a qualification in programming or computer technology, but needs enough expertise to overcome the jargon and to overcome a natural tendency to be overawed by technical procedures. Indeed, not all members and officials need the training. A specialist department, probably part of research, can do the job adequately enough. Unions will have to face this sort of future if they are to protect the interests of their members. As commerce and industry learn to use the computer so unions will have to learn to oppose it – not negatively, but to prevent what will undoubtedly otherwise be its capacity for exploitation.

Chapter 12

Shaping society

Concorde has succeeded in making the world a far smaller place and is undoubtedly the forerunner of faster travel. In a very short space of time satellite telecommunication equipment has brought people closer together and revolutionised communications between different countries. The computer now solves complex problems in seconds rather than the years they would have taken. Indeed the last decade has seen a vast technological change altering our conception of time, distance and speed and the computer has played an integral part in all of this. However, there is far more that the computer has done in a quieter, structural way. Rather like when people think of imports they concentrate on the finished consumer goods such as cars, refrigerators and electronics and tend to forget that the majority of imported manufactured goods are components, screws, hinges, etc., so the effect of the computer, when it is not providing a final goal or service, is forgotten.

Computers are extremely potent tools. Their ability to handle complex problems swiftly and to analyse data in ways not previously practicable in the time available has meant that whole new ranges of concepts have come into play. Other areas which had been exploited in only a rudimentary fashion have been developed to something approaching their latent potentialities.

Although one can hardly call the machine the same in all instances, computers have revolutionised telecommunications, designing and business-efficiency and made space exploration possible among other general uses. The machines have ranged from the mini-computer to the huge banks of large computers; all that they have in common, other than the name, are their properties of speed and accuracy. Yet it is these properties which mark out computers as special tools, not quite in the normal run of machine development. They more than extend a person's inherent physical capabilities, as, for example, a car extends the walking or running capability, or an electron microscope extends sight. They act as an extension of the mental facilities, not by being a particularly clever brain in themselves but by speeding up what would be normal brain processes. Computers are the only range of machines which do this and as such must be considered as a different development to all others, however sophisticated they may be.

Earlier in the book we mentioned the centralising potentialities of computers and this is a factor which must be explored in more detail as it has very important implications. The computer can enable enterprises to grow merely because of the capacity to store and analyse gigantic amounts of disparate information, information that is stored centrally and on which centralised decision-making depends. All organisations have to take decisions and decisions can only be taken in the light of information received at the time, and the guesses (intelligent or otherwise) based on this information. Where information is, decisions are made: if information is collected, stored and analysed centrally then that is where decisions will be taken. Those who make the decisions also, by definition, control the enterprise (unless financial management is undertaken by a third party) and thus control becomes centralised. This dual consequence of increased unit size and increased centralisation has had deleterious effects on management–labour relations and on the relationships between the electorate and those elected, for in both instances remoteness accompanies the structural changes. These, however, are broad, wide-ranging points. Within this general statement are specific examples of change; on the one hand the growth of certain procedures and enterprises and on the other hand the decline of some others.

The concentration of industry and commerce is the major noticeable feature and with it the growth of conglomerates. A conglomerate company is difficult to define but is basically a holding company under whose umbrella are various separate companies whose final goods or services have little in common with each other. This is a relatively new trend. The history for company mergers has generally been for one company to merge with, or takeover, other companies whose output was complementary or supplementary to their own. The conglomerate works on the principle that business is business no matter what; it is concerned with profit and return to capital and that alone, no matter what means be used to maximise this return in the short term. Although this may sound a damning and indeed sweeping indictment, recent history has shown this to be the rule rather than the exception. The computer, as a tool, is invaluable in this type of business approach.

A conglomerate company may typically include such diverse companies as insurance, car hire, electronic, heavy engineering and leisure provision. Both to determine the rates of return to capital invested, and thus to analyse the capital used in relation to its market value in a multi-company conglomerate, needs computer time and expertise if the enterprise is to be treated as a single entity. There are, however, two distinct ways of managing such a concern. The first is to keep a very tight rein, standardise statistics and refer all financial and development matters back to the central organisation, while the second is to allow a great deal of autonomy to the individual companies in their own markets, providing that they meet pre-determined profit targets.

In either case, the computer must play an important part in working through the calculations which will determine the group return. On the acquisition side, the holding company will undoubtedly subject the accounts, corporate plans, market potential, asset development and other factors to a detailed scrutiny before deciding where to purchase, and at what price to purchase. Given that the holding company may have multiplicity of different accounting systems and accounting years to cope with, it may have to standardise systems and the only practicable way is by using data-processing. It may be an accident that the growth of conglomerates runs parallel with the growth of computer use. It is possible, however, that the conglomerate has been created by computers in the sense that without them they would be impossible to control internally effectively.

The normal takeover or merger situation similarly relies on the computer for effective information. This is, of course, not to assert that takeovers are not possible without computers – that, patently, is nonsense – what it does assert is that the computer had made takeovers easier to occur and allowed the ensuing logistics of the merger to be handled more efficiently. This form of integration generally works vertically. That is, through product processes as opposed to the horizontal method used by conglomerates. Vertical integration is the logical development of an industrial and commercial system and invariably ends with an oligopolistic or even monopolistic market situation.

Vertical integration requires, if carried out efficiently, a considerable degree of planning and coordination in areas as diverse as production, transport and marketing. When intermediate product companies are small and deal with a handful of customers, and the final product produced has only a small share of the total market, such conditions could easily be handled by a clerical team. Nowadays all the companies involved are large and complex in themselves, depend considerably on the supply of imported fuels and raw materials and on Government legislation to determine consumer market levels. Without computers to handle the calculations and to produce the optimum organisation needed the even larger bodies that integration brings about would be unmanageable.

Both the conglomerate and the very large corporation have important repercussions on the trade unions and their work. Vertical integration certainly makes a company more vulnerable for an industrial dispute – it makes for a 'higher profile'. The interdependence of one plant upon another's output has always existed but the linking of plants to get complementary production schedules has heightened the dependency. The result is that any dispute affecting a supplier-part of a large concern can directly affect the output and, indeed, the employment in the end-product plants. While this gives far greater leverage to the unions in a bargaining sense it also brings its own disadvantages. In the last analysis an employee has only one weapon to use against an employer, and that is withdrawal or modification of his or her labour. In recent years we have seen an increased Press and TV coverage of disputes and often the stories of the type 'fifty men hold Leyland to ransom', a typical example of what vertical integration can do in industrial relations terms. No one likes striking, money is lost and the average employee is hard-put to withstand the loss, yet people like even less the prospect that their actions affect the livelihood of other employees. This acts as a moral constraint on workers. The second point in this situation is that both the media coverage and the statistics on working days lost through dispute actions concentrate on the third-party effects. The unions have had virtually no chance to play any part in the reorganisation of industry which has led to this state of affairs. Both the increasing dependence on expensive capital equipment (including computers) and the vertical integration are the main culprits. To blame the unions is to deny their right to take any action in their own defence – a denial that only totalitarian regimes will condone.

The conglomerate company poses slightly different questions to trade unions. The first is 'who controls what?' A union negotiates with what it believes is the employer and finds that negotiations are actually being controlled by a third party, physically and spiritually sheltering many miles away – (and with a financial personality tucked away in a tax haven?). As a result, the negotiations tend to be protracted, pointless and ultimately lead to unsatisfactory conclusions for both sides. Corporate policy is decided in an environment totally distinct from the work-place and managers themselves are placed in the position of being errand-boys in relation to trade unions, and often their own subordinates. This does nothing for either the confidence of the manager or the confidence of those who have to carry out his orders.

The drift towards largeness in the commercial, financial and industrial centres is followed by the public services. Central government departments have become larger, embracing as sub-departments what were previously ministries in their own right. Local government has been reorganised into units which are now so large that 'local' is a misnomer and the Health Service has lost any local accountability that it ever had. A bold statement that all this is due to the computer cannot be justified but how could all the administrative problems associated with these changes have been solved without data-processing? Could, in fact, these changes actually have been even contemplated if those who decided on them had not realised that tools such as the computer existed and would be able to solve the problems? Probably not. The next question is, have any of these Government structural changes had a beneficial effect either through increased efficiency, increased services, increased participation or better industrial relations? Sadly the answer to all these must be 'no'.

While there has been this concentration of domestic power controls there has also been a growth in international concentration; the growth of the multi-national corporation whether conglomerate or not is a feature of the 1960s and 1970s. If running a modern industrial giant company on a national basis is difficult, the multi-national multiplies these difficulties several-fold. The advantages for the owners are correspondingly increased as are the problems posed to the trade unions. Multi national companies are the dominant feature of British industrial life, whether British, foreign, or jointly owned. Their impact has been considerable enough for there to have been a US Senate investigation of their methods, a United Nations' enquiry into their power and to have spawned a huge and menacing literature; in themselves they have given birth to a secondary industry of observation.

A major worry, to governments and individuals, is the existence of large dominant companies in countries around the world which owe no allegiance to the countries in which they are nominally home-based. They do not have, and often do not bother to claim, social or economic responsibility to those countries, avowing that their responsibility, in global terms, is to their shareholders, which is often an euphemism for the ruling oligarchy. The result of this can be seen clearly in several instances. The Chrysler manoeuvres in 1975 with a threatened pull-out of Britain, the BLMC closure of the Innocenti plant in Italy, the acquisition and closure of Imperial typewriters by Litton Industries are examples of the power a multi-national deploys. In most cases there is not even any reason why the company should lose its market share in the country from which it withdraws, it just switches its production to a plant in a different country and fills the vacuum by importing its own products.

Transfer-pricing between different countries and plants is another anti-social practice. In essence it is the selling of a product from a plant in country 'A' to a plant in country 'B' at artificially high or low prices. Examples of this system are difficult to cite because the practice is nominally illegal in Customs and Excise terms. However, the Hoffman La Roche case concerning Librium and Vallium before the Monopolies Commission threw up the extraordinary prices that the British plant was paying for the vital ingredients to Hoffman La Roche companies in other countries. This meant that the company were probably taking their profits outside Britain to countries where, perhaps, the rate of corporate taxation was lower. The reverse situation can also prevail, which is selling, for example, a car engine to a foreign subsidiary at a low cost so minimising the profit in Britain (even perhaps making a loss) and taking the profit in the receiving country. The multi-national corporation sees its profits in world terms and will attempt to reduce its tax liabilities legally by such methods even though they may have artificially distorting effects on the balance of payments of a country and the serious consequences that this might have. The computer matters critically in this area.

As with other centralisations and conglomerations, it has a catalytic action, especially in multi-national terms. Companies such as ITT, if literature on the company is to be believed, use standardised information procedures and are subject to tight internal control mechanisms, this control being exercised by the American leaders at regular meetings. Both the standardisation and control would be infinitely more difficult, not to say impossible, without the use of computers directly and their use in telecommunications indirectly. In cases where the control is far less stringent a multi-national corporation still has to coordinate its production and sales, its research and patent policies and has to determine exactly where, when and how it will take its profits, again, an exercise in which the computer needs to play a considerable part. While the computer plays this role, unions cannot reasonably expect multi-nationals to fail or diminish in number, rather, the reverse will be true. As exploiters of capital and labour, they have the inestimable advantage of being able to finance more research, gain access to markets, pressurise governments and perhaps even bring down governments.

Trade unions have a great interest in the future of multi-nationals on two levels, that of domestic collective bargaining procedures and that of their effect on economic life as a whole. Multi-nationals have a bad record (comparatively) when recognising trade unions, one of the worst offenders being in the computer manufacturing industry. Even when recognition has been granted, the multi-national uses bargaining tactics which may reasonably be described as unfair, if not downright anti-social. The first is the pleading of poverty and low profits, which, in the context of transfer-pricing and global profit-taking is often quite laughable but the problem is that under present British Company Law the accounts which have to be made available to unions or the public do not reveal such practices. The second point is the threat that the company will remove its investment to a lower wage country, although it is getting difficult to find lower wage countries than Britain. Some years ago Henry Ford felt the need to visit Britain during a strike to make such a statement and although the threat is rarely carried out because of the loss of capital that such an action would entail, if it were to be carried out it would be because of the essential unprofitability of the operation rather than strikes.

In a strictly logistical sense there are difficulties for trade unions and managements when negotiating. All too often the responsibility for offers, counter offers and other decisions will not or cannot be taken by the British management and clearance and guidance has to be obtained from the parent organisation. This would not matter overmuch if it just entailed lifting a telephone and having a chat; it does matter considerably when the telephone call has to span continents and inter-continental time differences are in operation.

Trade-unionists appreciate that better wages and conditions can only be obtained if the total amount of profit or revenue is sufficient, or perhaps will be sufficient. Hence, unions are interested in the performance of the economy as a whole, because isolated institutions or companies cannot, in the long run, prosper in a declining system. The asset-stripping 1960s (and in hindsight those heroes of the social and business columns have so much to answer for) have given way to the contracting corporate combination 1970s. Britain has set itself on a course of larger, integrated units, of international, political, economic and business ties combined with a diminishing stock of manufacturing industry capital. This combination is, and must be, a disastrous recipe for the well-being of employees and of all but a handful of companies and currency dealers. The computer has had a large part to play in this rapid decline over the last one-and-a-half decades; certainly, the trend was evident well before, but the acceleration has been disturbing. Other countries have not had such a decline. Germany, the USA, Japan and France all use data-processing techniques to the same extent, if not more so, than Britain yet have not had the same unfortunate results. This may well be due to the fact that they use their computers for different managerial purposes; they don't superimpose them on declining industries; both managers and employees have a different ethos in Britain and the British market historically (since the First World War) has demanded a high rate of short-term distributed profits. It is not, therefore, inevitable that the situation in Britain should be echoed elsewhere, although left-wing social critics could argue that the computer has only speeded-up an inevitable decline.

If there are new structures and changed circumstances within the fabric of national life so the trade-union movement has to adjust itself to those changes. If companies or departments merge the relevant union organisations must merge, as unions are end-oriented in their short-run work. If multi-national corporations expand and dominate, so the trade unions must set up parallel organisations. No single national trade-union centre can adequately deal with multi-national companies and having realised this a group of international trade secretariats, already in existence but on primitive levels have set about organising world-wide company-based committees. The most advanced of these are in the chemical and motor-car production industries, although union collaboration in transport has, in its way, probably been the most effective for the longest time. The differences of language and culture, political bias and affluence make such organisations both difficult to control and to take effective actions; at present the union side is but a faint, blurred and somewhat crumpled carbon copy of the world-wide company structure. The international secretariats suffer from at least one gravely serious defect, that of lack of cash. They cannot afford computers in an area where they are vital, they rely on the goodwill and work of individual national unions, who are most probably overworked domestically and because of this they have a communication problem.

This trend to centralisation and trans-national liaisons has reached its apotheosis with the formation of the European Economic Community. Not only does this encourage the formation of European companies, it is, in effect, a gigantic bilingual bureaucracy apparently united by a fervent desire to codify the uncodifiable, extinguish the remnants of national individuality and destroy forests to feed its appetite for paper-work. It too, depends heavily on the computer, as, indeed, all large concerns must do, and as it delves deeper into the trivia of turkey-dressing and the sex life of the hop so its data-banks must expand. Unions have even more of a problem when confronting the EEC than they do with multi-national corporations. Individual unions are impotent, only trade-union centres such as the TUC have any import and this has to be through either a trans-national union centre, the ETUC or EEC committees which are advisory only. Trade unions thus become emasculated in precisely the same manner as an individual company in a tightly controlled multi-national conglomerate corporation. Once again, the computer does not make this inevitable but the logic underlying the EEC which depends on the computer for its workability dictates this approach.

Western society has certainly been changed by the computer but what of the developing countries? Computers are expensive because they not only have a high initial capital cost, but they also require training facilities for staff and high-running and secondary costs. This pre-supposes that the Government can afford to run the electrical and other systems or that the private sector can do so. Few, if any, of the developing countries can have the capability now or in the near future to train a sufficient number of people and few, if any, of those Governments have the resources to use but a fraction of the computer time that an industrialised country uses. Furthermore, almost by definition there is only a small manufacturing sector. There is a theory which states that, especially in times of world inflationary pressures, the gap between the rich and poor countries increases. One symptom of this is an information gap. If the rich sector of the world holds most of the data-banks and does the research the gap becomes self-perpetuating, not only is it effective now, it becomes effective in the future. Information collected today becomes the basis for action tomorrow. In a real sense the computer is concentrating the wealth of the world and in global terms this could ultimately have the most serious repercussions.

This chapter has so far dealt with the changes in the structure of society and has dealt with ideas on a national or international basis. One does not, however, have to be a populist to recognise that economics and politics and, indeed, history, are about people. What this chapter has done is really to ignore people and to look at aggregates and averages. The nature of data-banks, of policies taken in the light of vast information deposits, of centralised government and business decision-making makes it far more likely that individual needs are overlooked and that minority interests are not met. The proliferation of interest groups in Britain, one-parent families, mental health, recidivists, all bear witness not only to increasing social problems but to a society which is incapable of dealing with them in the normal run of events.

Computer staffs are no doubt responsible people as socially aware as any group yet their jobs reduce individuals to a cipher. This, of course, need not be so. Programs could be developed to isolate the hidden needs rather than bury them, and this becomes yet again not a problem associated with the computer *per se* but with those who control it. Within the structural changes in society there have been immense personal changes of job, job content and life-styles, some people have benefited, others have lost.

From time to time television produces quasi-scientific programmes which nearly always have a sequence showing the latest university cybernetics department's toy, a robot which does amusing things. Although we are still years away from the robotisation of ordinary work, the robot bomb disposal methods have certainly saved lives and many machines, although not exactly robotic, are replacing humans. Bomb disposal, for example, is a case where everyone (with the exception of the bomber) agrees that this is a good use of a robot, but in other cases there will undoubtedly be those who disagree, generally those whose jobs have been lost. Computer sciences within universities are growing in importance and sophistication but an underlying question must be 'for whom is the research being done?'

Many jobs are downright dangerous, dirty, boring or otherwise unpleasant. Many lives are lost in mining operations, both from accidents and disease, in deep-sea fishing, in the handling of asbestos and other materials and, indeed, from diseases such as hepatitis among medical staffs. If computer technology could advance to the state of removing these jobs from the range of human activities there would still be some opposition from those concerned but only because society has not offered alternative employment. The same applies to drudgery in jobs. We have looked at the changes in job content consequent upon computerisation in the clerical and shop-floor areas. Whether or not there is opposition to the installation depends in great measure on the change that the installation brings to jobs and job-prospects.

In an ideal society people would only do what they wanted to do and would only work when they wanted to. Although dubiously practical in a highly organised society, it is true that too many people work at things they do not enjoy and at times they least like. Boredom at work can be as the result of automation. Too often this is the case but automation and computerisation can, if handled skilfully, remove more drudgery than they create. As we have moved into the era of the giant concern, so the decisions affecting job content have inexorably receded away from the points at which most of the jobs are done, and new processes are developed, by research, with little or no thought given to those who will have to operate them.

Each change has brought about its problems, its boredom or its relief but these were incidental to the grand design; at the moment we are all fobbed off with consumer goods as the reward for tolerating the changes and unions have played their part in this system. Whether the Third World will allow us to continue along this road, even if we all wish to, is debatable. The computer offers the chance to change the whole system and in the next chapters we will discuss this and related matters.

Chapter 13

Who benefits: Them or us?

Computers are here to stay but, quite what they will do and for whom is still shrouded by considerable uncertainty. The technological changes which have been brought about by the computer, and the related mechanisms within organisations, will certainly change as the technology changes but in the last analysis it is unlikely that the clock will be turned back to pre-computer days. The processes are not reversible and cannot just be abandoned, if, for no other reason than the steep cost involved in so doing. The beauty of technological change is the dramatic impact that breakthroughs can make on standards and ways of life, and the uncertainties surrounding changes. Whether or not benefits of computerisation are distributed equitably depends on the organisation of industry and commerce and the uses to which computers are put.

In the course of this book we have explored the changes that have taken place, how they affect society and unions, in general and in particular, in the aggregate and as far as individuals are concerned. It is clear that society has not fully adjusted to computers, nor for that matter have trade unions and, what is worse, nor have the users themselves. There is a vast amount of under-use of capacity and an even larger under-use of potential, users appear to have neither the wit, nor the drive to exploit the machine's capabilities. To use large installations merely for payrolling and other simple clerical functions, as so many users do is tantamount to using a Maserati car to deliver mail in a congested city centre; it is a use, but hardly optimising the natural capabilities of the machine.

Industrialised society can be run on very different lines as the different political systems around the world show so well. The market or capitalist system, which in nearly all cases involves a publicly-owned sector; a centrally planned and directed Communist system; a more decentralised Communist system as in Yugoslavia, and the Scandinavian or British mixed economy. Each system has something to be said for it, each suffers from drawbacks and each has a different set of aims and objectives and in each the computer can play an important role. There is nothing inherent in the machines themselves that disqualify them or invalidate them from working in and then maximising the social objectives of any system. We have, however, argued that the natural tendency is for the computer to centralise decision-making through its centralisation of data unless definite positive steps are taken to reverse the situation. The trouble is that such steps involve the setting up of extra-mechanisms probably involving the use of more expensive on-line facilities which in accountancy terms may be an unjustifiable expense. The stress is on the word accountancy because the computer, above all other machines is the one which shows up our lack of a social accounting system in stark relief.

If the ingestion of tranquillisers is any measure of the happiness of a population (in inverse ratio) then the collective state of the British mind is not over healthy. Stress diseases, at least those that can be properly identified as being stress-related are, from the available, albeit sketchy evidence, on the increase. Yet the standard of living has never before been as high nor welfare benefits so widespread. People cannot at present cope with the strains, the pace or the targets set by our consumer society, or at least that appears to be one of the major problems. Foremost in this society is the myth that the consumer is sovereign and that consumer goods are measures of a man or woman's success. The computer, by making some processes more efficient, has theoretically been in the forefront of the great push forward. The 'quality of life', a much used but ill-defined phrase is really what this argument is all about; a feeling that all our yesterdays were better is abroad in Britain.

Although intangible, non-scientific and non-quantifiable, the problem is, nonetheless real and in some instances acute. Sociologists have tried to discover the causes, they acknowledge the existence of the phenomenon but as in all these cases the only common thread is the marked differences in opinion between the experts. Much of the isolation of individuals in society can be traced back to the inability of people to control their own destinies, as though the world was manipulating them rather than vice versa. A part of this must be due to the inflexibility of political and economic systems but another part due to sheer size, of buildings, roads, political and governmental institutions and enterprises. The computer has played a great part in this size build-up. We have argued that the computer's role to date in shaping society has been this stimulation of gigantism which, although theoretically at least it also enables economies of scale to be made, does bear with it this large social cost.

Who then benefits from computer use? If a computer enables a good or service to be produced more efficiently and more cheaply one of three things can happen in a market economy such as Britain's. The price to the consumer can drop or the producer may make larger profits or a combination of the two can occur. It is very difficult to isolate the various production costs in any one process; although the price may have risen the producer may legitimately argue that it would have risen far more had it not been for automated processes or other computer usage. The trick is probably that in some instances prices are held down and that in most instances profits are increased. If this were not so what would be the incentive to install computers, other than for an industry leader to install one and thus create a comparative advantage for itself, forcing the rest of the industry to catch up? This must inevitably lead to greater concentrations of wealth for those who produce; profits can only be made at the expense of consumers and most consumers are employees or former employees. It is by no means immutable that such wealth remains inequitably distributed; wealth and capital transfer taxes are perfectly comparable with a market economy. The system relies upon the attitude taken by most employers that increases in efficiency or productivity consequent upon computerisation should not be passed on to the employees as this is a return to fixed capital alone.

So, the consumer may benefit to the extent that some prices are lower than they would have been but, at the same time, salaries are lower than they might be, given the increased output. Thus the consumer-employee (one and the same person) is directly passing on foregone salary to profits but probably maintaining or even marginally increasing his real income. It does not take a genius to realise that such a system starts to hiccup rather badly if economic growth is not maintained; in City terms it is a technologically high gearing. It is not only the computer that creates this economic problem, all high technology, capital intensive industries do so.

As we have seen, however, the computer does have other benefits. Goods which previously were out of the price range of the majority of employees can be produced in sufficient quantities to drop the price in real terms, for example, television receivers. Credit itself becomes more easily available at reasonable interest rates given the lessening of risk factors which follow from more accurate information reaching the credit company. Telecommunications have certainly reached a new pinnacle of accuracy and speed with even greater developments to come, and we are still in the foothills of total computerisation. On the social wages side, job placement is becoming more efficient and once teething troubles are ironed out the personal services such as driving licence issuing, benefit claiming and rate collections will become equally so. As with Newton's Law that for every action there is an equal and opposite reaction so for every benefit there is a cost.

In Britain these costs are social ones, larger organisations, restrictions of consumer choice, remoter government, breaches of personal privacy, and the 'in work' problems that were discussed earlier. In any other form of political society there are also social costs, for example, the computer's ability to store and retrieve information as well as its use in communications make totalitarian regimes that much more viable. Those societies who against the odds are trying to decentralise industry and government find themselves, in the present technological state of the computer, being forced back into a position of central decision-making.

The question is whether such maldistributions of wealth and such social costs are inevitable or whether they are just a short-term result of producing a new tool which, more than any other yet invented (except for nuclear energy) has the power to change society. Taking the optimistic view the latter is probably the case. There are signs, some slightly more visible than others, that the major users of computers, central governments, are starting to realise that problems exist. Scandinavian countries, notably Sweden, have enacted privacy laws, Britain itself produced the Younger Report and now has a White Paper with a promise of similar legislation and even the European Economic Community has recognised that a problem exists quite separate from the problems of competing with IBM on the manufacturing side. Even if all the promises of action are put into practice and the genesis of recognition flowers into full cognisance only some of the problems will have been approached.

Governments can hardly take a legislative Luddite position and outlaw centralised data-banks and decision-making, for even if it were practicable they would be destroying a considerable amount of their own power. The answer here lies in technological development. The large computer has died away since the inception of the machine, but, in the same way that the development of the transistorised portable radio released people from the confines of the fixed set and aerial in a room, so the development of computers will be in the peripheral, mini-, on-line, real-time side. An EEC document *Community Policy for Data Processing* suggests strongly that this will be the big growth area, a growth which will be at the expense of growth in the large installation market.

If these predictions are correct, and they must be treated with some degree of caution given the poor record of forecasting in the data-processing sector by all commentators as well as being premissed on artificially high growth rates, fundamental changes will be possible. A multiplicity of mini-computers, linked or as terminals with their own storage facilities, opens up the possibility of the dissemination of information rather than central collection; opens up areas of devolving responsibilities rather than vesting them in fewer and fewer people. The silicon chip, advances in telecommunications and the powerful cheap mini-computers have all conspired to bring about the possibility of the first new computer revolution; the model T age is dawning. But this in itself will not be sufficient to reverse the process.

Senior managers of companies, mandarins in the Civil Service and multi-national corporation officers all have vested interests in maintaining their personal prestige and power and thus restricting, if not the abilities, then the use of this new wave of computers. Like governments, their first instinct will almost certainly be to place restrictions on the use of terminals by having limits on the programs' ability to get information from central sources or to maintain their own data-banks. It is here that trade unions come into the picture.

One of the major aspirations of unions is for their members, if not control, then to have, full participation in the enterprise in which they work. In the large multi-plant, multi-product company each company or plant in the group appears to the employees to work autonomously, even though they realise it is part of a larger whole. This dichotomy is explained by the remoteness of the central group and often the very large size of the single plant. If, for example, you ask a Rover car employee for whom he works, the reply will usually be 'Rover' and not BLMC. Given this tendency to identify and the need for trade unions to get localised, non-aggregated information, the pressure will be on to make full use of the new computer technology. On the surface this will yet again appear to be a direct confrontation between the company and unions but in this instance there will probably be a great difference. The management of the plant will also have a vested interest in getting the decentralised system in order to maximise their own power and decision-making responsibilities so that the confrontation will be between the component parts of a group and the central corporate body. Ultimately this may affect even multi-national information flows, which, so far, are remarkably one-sided.

The spread of industrial democracy legislation and worker directors should affect this fundamentally but meantime there are of course logistical problems and it would be foolish to ignore them. No one plant or company in a group can take decisions unilaterally which, on a group basis, not only conflicts with overall policy but may harm the prospects of other workers of that group. This danger does not depend on the type of ownership; whether privately or publicly owned, the same difficulty can arise. We must then evolve a joint decision-making process, with checks and balances but more equitable in the sense that power is more evenly distributed as well as wealth or income.

Apart from the problems hitherto described the computer has, either directly or indirectly, added to the stress/strain syndrome. Visits to doctors with what are thought to be stress-related symptoms are not made on the basis of philosophical insights into the running of a capitalist system or the recognition that computers are involved. Stress is a very personal syndrome and the adage 'one man's stress is another man's challenge' means that investigations into stress at work are bedevilled by uncertainties and often by the value judgements of the investigators themselves. Nevertheless signs and symptoms of stress diseases with physical manifestations are on the increase as are those with purely cerebral effects and tranquillisers are being prescribed in ever increasing numbers. It is difficult, if not impossible, to determine whether the causes are from the work or the home environment. However, strain or stress (strain is probably the more descriptive word) is, if reports by members of all unions are to be believed, on the increase in the work-place and now accounts for a considerable percentage of sickness leave.

The causes are multifarious. Boredom on a production line, noise and other hostile environments, pressure from keeping up with fast-moving lines, responsibilities which people have thrust upon them but are unwilling or incapable of taking are all part of the shop-floor phenomena. Dentists suffer strain through inflicting pain, some doctors are affected through having responsibility for lives, financial responsibilities affects some managers, while employment responsibilities affects others. Shift work, night work, sheer dislike of the job, overwork (especially among women workers who often have to maintain a household too) all play their part alongside the better-known manifestations of the phenomena among directors and senior management.

Computers, by their changing of processes and their centralisation of decision-making, have added to stress and strain. No one has yet documented a situation where a management has taken medical advice as to the impact that computer-inspired production changes may make on their work-force, before the changes are made. Employees are treated as pieces of all-purpose equipment, interchangeable and like other machines capable of being worked to destruction, with the National Health Service providing the periodic servicing and repairs. People are fortunately not machines. There also are other reasons why computers have added to strain at work, some of which have already been touched upon.

The technical nature of the computer cuts off the majority of people from its mysteries and disqualifies them from taking any part in the decision-making process. By the same token some jobs have been changed, and as time and technology advance, will continue to change, and with new expertise needed to continue this process. As we get more computer-controlled production processes so the need to monitor the process spreads further down the managerial ladder and the skills needed filter down. Indeed, in the computer knowledge chain, there is most often a jump from data-processing staff to line management with general senior and middle management missed out. This places extra responsibilities on employees such as foremen who as first-line management have the duty to ensure that their section of production is working smoothly. In an automated or computer-controlled process this will entail a knowledge of the system without which the supervisor cannot sometimes spot a fault and certainly wouldn't be able either to rectify it or to take some form of compensatory action. Increasingly, graduate foremen are being hired by large companies, often as a first step on the road to the senior management, if they prove to be good enough. This enables a company to acquire the newer techniques knowing that at the direct production end there is enough knowledge to cope with the demands of the system. However, as we mentioned earlier, this has been achieved at some considerable cost, a cost that has not yet reached the point where it has become noticeable but when it does will have real social implications.

The present recruitment area for (say) engineering foremen is among charge-hand grades and these are promoted from those on the shop-floor. In an ordinary large engineering enterprise with the normal amount of labour turnover it takes an employee about 4 years to become a charge-hand and 6 to 7 to become a foreman, assuming he or she wishes to do so and lets the employer know it. On average again a foreman supervises the work of about eight other employees so that there is a minimum 12½ per cent chance of promotion to first-line management levels and given labour mobility the chance must be nearer 20 per cent. If, as we suggest and indeed the process has started, foremen have to cope with critical-path analysis techniques and be able not only to read print-outs but also to ask the correct questions to get the print-out in the first place, it is asking a great deal of a promoted shop-floor employee with no electro-mechanical calculating or computer background. Although the number of combinations of actions delegated to the foreman will be of necessity limited, the job becomes less of an extension of his original shop-floor work and more a technical occupation needing a different basic or higher education. This disqualifies many shop-floor employees and consequently cuts out the only available promotion opportunity for most employees. In turn this means either changing jobs completely or coming to terms with a life on the shop-floor. Neither option gives much hope for advancement in the future for many millions of employees.

This freezing of the vertical mobility which has prevailed for so long in Britain is paralleled by the difficulties that graduates have had in recent years in getting the jobs to which they thought they were entitled. More and more are now looking at the supervisory grades as that *entré* into the managerial élite for which they are qualified. It is as though in military terms the sergeant suddenly became a trainee officer. However, there are now less shop floor employees, for it is commerce, government, health services and the staff sections of industrial companies that provide the bulk of employment in Britain today. Additionally, of course, there are the professions and the self employed.

As technology changes so new skills are needed to run and service the new equipment and with judicious retraining and the training of the young this can be done. More important are both those whose existing and specific skills are made obsolete and those whose general and non-specific skills are replaced. A young man or women joins an employer full of hope and ambition, not necessarily with the notion of becoming managing director or first secretary but hoping to advance as far as possible in the world. To this end skills are acquired at school and perhaps in further education. If, as a result of change totally outside the control of the individual these chances are either completely or drastically reduced what incentive is there to work harder or more conscientiously? To be specific how does a 30-year-old insurance industry employee feel when he sees his normal career pattern totally disrupted by the introduction of computerised policy return systems? His area of personal discretionary action has been curtailed making the job less interesting into the bargain. Obviously he does not feel overly well disposed towards the computer.

We must then return to the question, who benefits? For employees there is very often better health and safety. If computers can remove the necessity for manual testing of dangerous machines or noxious substances, that is all to the good. Computers or computer-controlled machines can do this and do indeed do so. No amount of money can compensate for drastic injury or chronic ill health so the benefit is, in all respects, unquantifiable. Automated detection devices in other forms of plants are also life-savers.

The same question applies to environmental and resource depletion considerations. We have all seen how the quintupling of the price of oil had such drastic effects on the economies of the world in inflation terms and in the restrictions that were then needed on the consumption of oil products. We live in a world of finite resources; that fact brooks no argument although there are arguments enough for what follows this basic statement. Some feel that market forces will always solve the problem, e.g. if a raw material starts to run out its price will rise and substitutes will be used; others pin their faith in recycling; others in technological advance;

some in innate optimism while the last category believes there is no hope other than zero growth. For all the pundits there is one common agreement, that the day of judgement or otherwise is well enough into the future for them all to die with their reputations firmly intact. As with the artificially induced price rises in oil, however, there is a serious depletion problem and one which computers can make a significant contribution in alleviating.

To minimise the consumption of materials one needs to be able to work in the most efficient way possible and thus minimise wastage. This computers can do far more easily than man. Secondly international agencies should be able to monitor both depletion and production techniques and thus guide the technological changes into threatened resource substitution paths. On the pollution side automatic monitoring devices can spot hazards before they build up and often the most efficient production technique is the least pollutive. This whole area is, however, fraught with difficulties about who pays for anti-pollution devices. Together with better health and safety the computer has contributed and can continue to contribute to the quality of life of people, but the question remains for what.

Earlier in the chapter we argued that unless political (in all senses of the word) initiatives were taken the tendency toward the centralisation of power would increase. Equally we argued that the computer would, certainly in a market economy such as Britain's, accentuate the inequities in wealth distribution – in other words to those that have computers would be given more money and thus more power. Not only would the advocates of social reform find this unacceptable in Britain, the average man and woman would find it both politically and socially abhorrent. Any democratically removable Government, whatever its political persuasion, will be forced by one means or another, to check this drift because the results will be so apparent as to be intolerable.

Corporate taxation will have to rise to siphon off the excess profits made and the resultant monies be distributed in the form of additions to the social wage. If this fails, and the opposition will be well organised, voluble and expensively mounted, then direct public participation or ownership will be the answer. If such actions are not taken and the benefits of the computer are allowed to accrue mainly to companies it will be a recipe for social disorder. Technological advances which create wealth should be for the benefit of all, not the very few and one which offers so much scope for wealth creation while having so many social costs attached to its use carries with it special responsibilities. It is not, however, something that Britain can do on its own or indeed can the Common Market manage. The multi-national companies with their global strategies can, in Britain, wreck the economy by simply moving away to continue where the pastures are greener, and Governments are both less scrupulous and concerned.

There is nothing quite so strange as the scientific communities' insistence that advances in their area are for mankind in general and the international symposia set up to exchange knowledge when compared with the indifference of the same scientists to the exploitation of their discoveries. This is matched only by the general public's lack of monitoring of such use of the discoveries. Most of the advances are made in the universities or institutions funded out of general taxation, yet for the most part those inventions are used to create more wealth for those who can afford to use or exploit them. Unfortunately as technological advance consequent upon scientific advance gets more sophisticated, so costs rise and create increasing barriers to entry and the difficulty of continuance in industry. This means that the number of manufacturers of the equipment tend to decrease and in turn with the reign of artificially high oligopolistically-administered pricing the number of prospective users also decreases; that is until, as we may now see with computers, second generation equipment rules otherwise. Even so, if the computer is to become a necessity for any enterprise to compete successfully it argues the squeezing out of the small entrepreneur in favour of the large corporation or unit; barriers to entry do not only affect manufacturers.

Although this applies to almost all technological advances it applies to the computer above all others. This is because its use is so widespread and its activities and potential so enormous. Thus not only does it aid concentration but it excludes those who competitively try to break in. It concentrates power, political and economic, within a single nation and between nations. It aids the multi-national companies in their efforts to escape their responsibilities to any one nation. In short it is, and will unless checked, continue to be a most divisive instrument. It could well be the tool that made capitalism work so well that the people upped and destroyed it – not the tool but capitalism. More probable, however, should that eventuality loom large on the horizon, is that steps will be taken to partially share the benefits, even if the costs remain very lopsidedly distributed; this has always been the pattern in Britain.

Chapter 14

Force for good or force for evil?

When kindly, worldly and humane Dr Jekyll first transmuted himself to ugly, extravagantly lecherous and treacherous Mr Hyde the reader was thrilled and shocked. Psychologists had a bench mark on which to formulate their ideas of the inner self hidden beneath the veneer of civilisation – the dark side of the moon as it were. This dichotomy of personality, has fascinated authors and playwrights down the centuries but has hardly even been attributed to machines for the simple reason that machines have no personality, no will of their own and are totally dependent on the operator. Yet many machines or substances have, over the ages, been used for both good and evil purposes depending on who was using them or ordering their use.

The bow and arrow which enabled man to progress in hunting and thus abandon full agrarian dependence also enabled wars to be prosecuted more efficiently, the gun and gunpowder showed the same facilities at a later date. The internal combustion engine, when put in cars and buses, opened up vistas and horizons then unknown to the working classes yet has claimed as its revenge the lives of hundreds of thousands, maimed considerably more and polluted the environment. The same gas used to kill rats has been used in Hitler's gas chambers to kill people, aeroplanes can bring families closer together or drop bombs on the self-same families, and nuclear power can bring cheap energy, conserve scarce natural resources or destroy civilisation as we know it.

The computer encompasses a range of machines, that, aside from the Armageddon effects of nuclear warfare – and even here it enables it to be more efficiently conducted – has by far the largest potential impact for good or for evil of any yet invented. It is tantamount to being the nucleic acid of a good or evil person; providing the genetic structure without which that person would not exist and would not be unique. The potential is all the more alarming given both the widespread use of computers and the lack of public knowledge of their activities and functions. Few people, in percentage terms, understand them, fewer still can make them work and fewer still control them. There is now a technological élite, not as yet dangerous because, certainly in Britain, no philosophy has arrived to control and coordinate their activities.

We have in the course of this book looked at the relationship between the computer and trade unions and in doing so had also to look from a committed viewpoint at society and the economy too, and must in passing have set some sort of record for any book purporting to have anything to do with computers by only using the world i*t*r*a*e once. We have looked at some uses and applications, noted the benefits and costs and explored the problems, some short term, others more long term and fundamental. Job costs and benefits, consumer costs and benefits, the problems in the industry itself and for data-processing people, all of them referred to in a trade-union context, as was the use of computers by the trade-union movement itself. Chapters 12 and 13, however, started to explore how computers have helped and are continuing to shape society and posed the most important question, who will benefit from them. This last chapter will continue in this vein because this is an under-explored, under-argued area, and one which must greatly exercise if not us, then our descendants.

It is not only whether computers will be used for good or evil in the classic result-orientated sense but whether they will be used to provide the greatest benefits for the greater number or to exploit the greatest number. Although both questions depend on who is using the computer and thus depend for their answers on the type of political system in operation, the second question is the more fundamental in society terms. Swindlers can easily use a computer and indeed have done so, in the United States on a substantial scale, although significant cases have been suppressed to avoid a loss in customer and user confidence. In most recorded cases the thefts have been discovered by accident.

As already stated technological advances have not always been used for good purposes – the civil uses for napalm are few and far between – yet most have advanced the cause of civilisation and mankind. Computers certainly come into this category in almost every single facet of life from cradle to grave – that is their unique quality. The basis of food, health, housing and income, the necessities of life can all be improved by the judicial use of computers, both in Britain and those countries which need the most dramatic improvements, the developing non-industrialised nations. Allocation of resources can be made more efficiently, the distribution of goods and services made more cheaply, Government administration reach new peaks of achievement, all with the aid of computers. Some of this has been achieved. Certainly life expectancy is rising and morbidity rates falling world-wide, although some countries have far further to go than others, and computers play an integral part in most medical and para-medical research.

The pre-computer days of the 1950s were the halcyon times of Harold Macmillan's 'you have never had it so good' yet since then people have ostensibly had it better. Real incomes have risen, more families own cars, some two or three, nutrition has improved (at least up to 1974), clothes changed more often, there are more fridges, more TV sets; in fact more consumer goods of all descriptions were purchased year by year until the cataclysmic years of 1975 and 1976. Once again the computer must have played its part, unquantifiable as it may be, in this building of affluence.

The costs, however, are beginning to be felt. Increases in psychological disorders, stress and strain diseases indicate some deeper seated problem.

Alienation in the work-place which has led to the strange remedy of 'job enrichment' premised an idea that somehow, something modest can be found to assuage fundamental problems; dissatisfaction fostered at home, for how else can you build up the pressure to replace still viable consumer durables or buy another non-essential product? Man may be naturally acquisitive yet the advertising industry gets through a lot of money to persuade him that he actually is; obviously manufacturers do not think that he knows his own nature.

There are breaches of confidentiality, unsolicited junk mailings; disturbing cases where personal privacy has been infringed. Computers have added to the natural confusion and turmoil at work where new techniques have cut off some employees from their established routines and added to the national stress aggregate. These are the effects to date but the point about computers is that we have hardly begun to explore their potential in either the uses to which they can conceivably be put or indeed in using the capacity of the existing stock of computer time making use only of known techniques. It is this unknown potential which is at the same time the most exciting and the most worrying.

As the potential benefits increase so do the potential dangers if only because the sheer amount of data held increases too. At the same time access to computers becomes the prerogative of fewer and fewer people although this danger might disappear if the new generation of equipment is based on the decentralising mini- or perhaps micro-computer as promised. The Government White Paper *Computers and Privacy* goes some way to recognising at least some of the dangers and recommends the setting up of a Data Protective Committee which will give advice to the Government on the intricacies involved in personal protection. For example, how open should records be to the individual concerned, especially medical records?, where, if records are open, does national security consideration start?, and so on.

These questions, important as they may be, actually beg the very fundamental questioning that will have to be made if and when computers start to be used more widely and more efficiently. Strangely Britain has an advantage in this respect. Although we were in the field very early we have fallen behind in applications and as a result have more time to avoid the pitfalls and a chance to learn from other people's mistakes.

The fundamental question is whether, in the last analysis, a capitalist society or market economy such as Britain's, albeit slightly mixed with public ownership, can adapt to the computer and ensure its own survival.

In other words, benefit or exploitation. History is littered with the debris of broken men sacrificed to the machines or processes in the name of profits, yet in almost all the instances the effect was localised; the computer is universally applicable. Why then is there such a possible conflict? It is what the computer may be able to do rather than what it has done that will cause the problems and so to analyse the position it is first necessary to rehearse the more likely effects.

Computers, computer technology and automated techniques can replace most of the jobs of most of the people for most of the time. Some jobs cannot be replaced, at least not until robots replace the drudge's work and computers become both cheap enough and sufficiently readily available to attempt general medical diagnosis. Other jobs which require value judgements as opposed to physical skills, knowledge of people as opposed to knowledge of things are irreplaceable. Service engineers will be in great demand, whole professions such as the law, surgery, dentistry, accountancy (described in the United States as a form of creative writing) will all survive intact although their aids will be that much more sophisticated. Despite the probable growth of office machinery, secretarial and clerical staffs will still be essential; despite automation men will still be required to observe and adjust processes and machines. We will still need some miners, people to man oil rigs, sit on, if not actually drive trains or pilot planes, except in emergencies; drive buses; taxis and cars; plough fields and herd the cows. Not everything can be computer-controlled and even if this were not so it would not be economically viable for many processes or jobs to be so controlled.

The service and economic infrastructure industries will be the least affected, the manufacturing sector change the most in terms of employment and work done. Some service industries could undoubtedly change very markedly. Banking, for example, could operate an automatic service to customers with employees only being used for the loans and securities departments, while others like the hairdressing or construction industries will still remain labour intensive. Skilled jobs in industry, the machinists, welders, etc., will be at great risk while the number of semi-skilled or unskilled jobs, although decreasing, will still be considerable. This is certainly not a science-fiction type of future, where everything is controlled by machines which even have machines to repair them, it is a restrained view of the early twenty-first century, a time when the majority of the people now living in Britain should still be alive.

What sort of society can support this high technology and low employment? We have argued that the computer has had little effect on the total of jobs available to date and this is supported by studies made in the USA, but this is unlikely to be the case for very much longer. The unfortunate joke of computer installations absorbing more people than they displace, although initially true, is now a thing of the past. Cost-effective management techniques have superseded the prestige-oriented growth patterns in data-processing, users have learned from their mistakes and the numbers of staff employed per installation has, if anything, decreased slightly since 1970. This method of soaking up the surplus labour created by installations will no longer be possible. So in all, more people, assuming constant birth and mortality rates (although life expectancy should rise over time, especially with medical computer use), will be chasing fewer jobs.

Such a situation can be resolved in many ways. There could be a high level of unemployment, higher than in the depression period of the 1930s, but only if the system ensures the same standard of living for both the unemployed and the employed – otherwise it will be totally unacceptable. There can be systems of work sharing. These can be of different types. For example there can be one week on, one off on a shift system or the working week be reduced to 2 or 3 days, again with a shift system or a working day reduced to 4 hours yet again with a shift system. All of these answers pre-suppose that those who own the means of production will deliberately and voluntarily reduce their profits by either paying the higher taxes necessary to fund unemployment pay at very high levels or by increasing their payroll unnecessarily. It also assumes that all the goods produced will be purchased and also that the employees are interchangeable between skills. The first premise may not be true, the second certainly is not. It also assumes a remarkable growth in leisure activities and presumably their associated industries.

The traditional view of computerisation is that because fewer people will be employed in the manufacturing processes and the back-up for them, the people so released will be able to man the hospitals, build the schools and houses, police the streets and work in other services now critically short of manpower. How do we employ a technologically unemployed labourer from Tyneside as a nurse in a hospital in Peterborough? Apart from the difficulties associated with mobility referred to earlier, that man would simply not have the skills required for such a job. This traditional view is dependent on the acceptance of the classical economic production function. In English this means that the level of production or output depends on a mix of capital and labour and that these two items are interchangeable. This is a patent nonsense. Not only are men and machines not interchangeable (they might just have been so in Adam Smith's day) but man is not interchangeable with man, by and large, and as specialisation and technical sophistication increases the scope for interchangeability becomes progressively less.

For the traditional view to prevail some decidedly non-traditional remedies must be implemented. There must, for instance, be a system whereby mobility is not only encouraged but made as easy as possible. The scale of the problem would dictate that the present-day attempts at encouragement using capital sum moving grants and rent subsidies over a limited period would be inadequate. Only a radical system of labour market planning plus municipalisation to create a surplus (and flexible) housing stock could provide a solution. Even so the British social system which mitigates against mobility would have to be overcome and if financial incentives failed a limited direction of labour might be the only answer. But who would advocate or accept that?

Training and retraining would have to be looked at completely afresh on a scale undreamed of in Britain, or indeed anywhere in the world so far. The best system is that in Sweden where it is limited to other employment services and strict notification of both impending vacancies and redundancies yet even here the maximum capacity is for only 3 per cent of the labour force at any one time. Britain has a so much smaller capacity for planning than this even after the preliminary and welcome work of the

Manpower Services Commission. The whole educational system will have to be recast because many of the jobs available will require real skills which the normal retraining schemes do not encompass. For example, medical educational facilities will have to be increased and provisions made for late entrants into medical schools and for para-medical training but this would demand a higher basic level of education than is at present provided. If the range and depth of retraining services are to be expanded to cater for a considerable percentage of the labour force at any one time (say 10 per cent), then the cost will be considerable and this again would mean even higher corporate taxation.

The emphasis is on corporate taxation because it is assumed that the computerisation will have meant increased profits and that although real incomes might be rising for those in work, the share of revenue going to profits will be increased. This is not an unreasonable assumption in the light of historical market-economy forces. One major problem would be that unless those unemployed are recipients of transfer payments there will be insufficient aggregate demand to maintain increasing levels of output and thus maintain profits and it is necessary for output to continue to increase. This is because the population will continue to increase and will need the extra food, goods and services. In addition capital-intensive industries have to meet fixed, generally high production levels to make a profit as there are few economies that can be made to cut costs, like cutting the labour force, in lean times. If one accepts that Britain will not be alone in these circumstances then any dreams of exports taking up the slack will be idle ones, unless these are made to developing countries. The traditional view also contains the notion that those released from productive labour will work in the service and leisure industries, but this also assumes a demand for these services and the problem of the unemployed's lack of purchasing power arises again.

Unless society is prepared to accept that those who do not work get the same income as those who do, or capitalism is prepared to accept work-sharing on a viable basis where real incomes for all continue to rise, thus reducing pre-tax profits, the system will collapse. Capitalism will also have to accept a higher burden of taxation to fund the unemployed or to provide a comprehensive retraining programme or perhaps both if society rejects these.

Consider then the alternatives that are open to a capitalist society in these circumstances. It can let unemployment rise and risk a collapse of the economy through lack of aggregate demand, a collapse which would be both accelerated and exacerbated by the high degree of capital intensity in the economy. As all other industrialised capitalist economies would be suffering from the same problems, to greater or lesser degrees, export-led recovery would not be sustainable over time and the economy would settle down to a lower plateau of incomes and expectations. In a world of rising expectations it is unlikely that such a situation would be tolerated and the existence of a very large unemployed, have-not sector would almost certainly guarantee some form of revolution. A variant on this would be for aggregate demand to be maintained by paying exceptionally high salaries to those who do work.

This would perpetrate a three-tiered system of those who own and have wealth and income, those who work and have high incomes and a heavy percentage of those who neither work nor have income. Again it is inconceivable that any democratic society could tolerate such a system; the inequities would be too glaring and in practical terms the have-nots would be too great a percentage of the population for any Government effectively to preside over the situation. Such a Government would have to be totalitarian in nature and almost certainly Fascist by political inclination.

The third alternative is for the system to take steps to distribute the benefits of technology. This would be by heavy corporate taxation reducing profits to levels, which certainly multi-national companies and probably domestic companies too would find unacceptable. The domestic company would have to 'grin and bear it', the multi-national would be constrained in its choices of movement by the fact that all industrialised countries faced similar problems and would have to go to those countries which opted for the Fascist road or some developing nations eager to welcome any form of investment. The income collected by taxation would have to be spent on retraining programmes, education, social welfare and non-employment salaries, health services and government services. This redistribution could also be made by companies paying a complete salary to employees working less than a full amount of work with employees working on a rota basis, so that there is more or less full employment at maintained income levels. This would in effect be a voluntary taxation policy by the company and would again decrease profits.

In time, there would, if this analysis is even half-way correct, be a critical decision point. Either the benefits of technology, especially computerisation, are equitably distributed or the State faces the possibility of violent lurches to either the extreme left or extreme right. Britain has never before faced such a decision, but certainly the national proclivity of at least two of its Common Market partners has shown them to be capable of embracing authoritarianism while a third turns to 'strong rulers' from time to time.

This will all take place, some considerable time into the future, but on the way to it problems will arise and have to be overcome and the way in which they are tackled will probably dictate the long-term future of the country. We have all been brought up in a *laissez-faire* type of society, to be sure not the nineteenth-century Liberalism type nor the twentieth-century Chicago School version but in a system where freedoms prevail up to a point and the market is allowed to work in a mainly untrammelled way, allocating labour, goods and services. As technological redundancies become more prevalent so the chances of maintaining this system diminish. There will almost certainly have to be administered pricing and this will probably include remuneration. The type of political system being maintained at the time will determine the trade-union responses to the situation; if it is even thought that wage restrictions are, in a situation like this, helping to maintain high profits there will be no chance of acceptance. Only a system which shows a genuine and, more important, effective desire to redistribute the newly created wealth can possibly persuade unions to accept such an administered society.

In all, the trade unions will have a difficult job in this period. Not unnaturally they will be trying to keep as many of their members in work as possible; employers, on the other hand will be trying to shed as many employees as practicable. Ultimately, the trade unions will have to settle for a system which will probably include very high redundancy payments combined with support payments, much higher pensions (a minimum of 70 per cent actual average earnings) at a retirement age of probably 50 for either sex. Combined with this will be an accelerating push towards a shorter working week and rota systems of work, probably 20 hours for the one and one month on, one off for the other, all of course on full pay. Merely because fewer facilities would be needed at the work-place it would pay an employer to accept work-sharing on full pay rather than insist that all employees report to work at the same time, at least half of them having a zero marginal product, i.e. producing nothing. Alongside the social retraining schemes needed to divert employees into the socially productive, but of necessity not profitable areas such as the health services, this union campaign will almost certainly run into a very hostile response. There could be prolonged disputes nationally, and at long last on a world-wide multi-national company basis. The reasoning behind the coherence between workers of different nationalities would be that if we, the British 'go under' today, they, the foreign employees, would go under the day after.

This interim period will, in some senses, be the most critical. It is really thus an optimistic forecast in that Britain will probably avoid any totalitarian system, although in all probability she will have to take the majority of manufacturing industries into public ownership, especially the multi-national section, because at the end of the day capitalism without private profit and thus wealth inequalities must die.

But even with a fair, equitable, as little centralised as possible, socialist system, based on majority consent, there will still be problems. The first is the Protestant work ethic. This ethic, the inspiration behind the Industrial Revolution, has been deeply ingrained since then in the British culture. Unions have forever proclaimed the right to work, as though work was somehow an end in itself rather than a means, mainly unpalatable, of getting income for both the necessities and luxuries of life.

Trade unions themselves may have to reeducate their own officers and members to adjust to shorter working hours and more leisure. The Government will not only have to run employment training schemes but also leisure training schemes for never before will the majority of people have had such an opportunity of prolonged leisure. Unless educated to direct their energies into worth-while personal occupations and unless recreational courses and facilities are provided time will hang heavy and become the great enemy of the new leisured classes.

Assuming all these problems can be overcome other problems remain. How to prevent the arms race escalating as Governments attempt to reduce unemployment by stimulating their armaments industry? How to avoid wars, in which the computer would play a singularly unhappy role, in order to use these armaments? After all you can't stock-pile forever. Would our trading partners allow us the luxury of a socialist or at the least very highly modified capitalist system if they themselves had drifted into a rigid State framework?

Computers are at the root, trunk, branch and twigs of the probable technological explosions. Either directly, or more subtly, through intervening processes and research and development breakthroughs they will affect our lives radically, unless, of course, their promise is a false one and there can be no further developments – a highly improbable state of affairs. Some employees will be in more boring occupations, others far more interesting; the problems of confidentiality can easily be overcome by enforceable legislation as can those of privacy. The shorter working week should help to ease alienation at work and a more easy-going society with better leisure facilities should ease the stresses and strains apparent in the home. Britain and other industrialised countries, if they so wish, could then be in a position to offer positive, concrete aid to developing countries. The health and education of the nation could be improved and a better life obtainable for everyone. This enlightened concept depends on the distribution of the benefits obtained by computers so that they can be used for the majority of people, and, as we have seen socialism of sorts is the only method by which this can be achieved. The concentration of power, the exploitation, the enhancement of totalitarian power are all there if we should take the wrong turning at an earlier date.

Britain led the world in abandoning the feudal system and entering into the merchant, artisan, tradesman eras. It led the world in constraining the absolute monarch and in the implementation of a parliamentary system of government. It led the world in the Industrial Revolution and this, combined with the use of our Empire, laid a basis for our standard of living today. Why then should Britain not lead again, into the Leisure Revolution? It is an attractive notion and one which combines all the latent aspirations of trade unionists with the capabilities of the computer and one suspects and hopes that, if any country is capable of achieving this breakthrough, it is Britain.

Index

Advisory, Conciliation and Arbitration Service (ACAS), 67, 73, 74
agreements, 72–3
approximation problem, 23
arbitration, 46–7, 73
Ariel computer system, 17, 27, 28
assessment and promotion, 96–7, 117–18
asset stripping, 3, 20, 39, 108
assumptions, 75–6
ASTMS, 41, 47, 53, 59, 62–4 *passim*, 71–2, 85, 87
Atomic Weapons Research Establishment, 65
AUEW, 87–9 *passim*
automated plant, 25, 78, 81–2, 83, 111, 117

banks, banking, 17, 26, 40, 81, 124
Bevan, Aneurin, 40, 63
'Black Cattle', 6
blackleg labour, 53
'black-list', 101
BLMC, 107, 115
bonus schemes, 8, 94–5
boycotts, 35
British Airways, 3
British Computer Society, 61, 63
British economic system,
  and computers, 113–14
  future prospects for, 74
  present development of, 38
  sections of, 10, 15–16
British Leyland, 16, 22
British Medical Association, 63
British Petroleum, 16
British Rail, 18, 27
British Steel Corporation, 11, 16, 65
building societies, 26
Burroughs, 64, 66

capital equipment, and productivity, 95
capital-intensive industries, 39–41, 43, 114, 126
capitalism, 126, 128
centralisation, 86, 90, 103–4, 109, 112, 114–16
Central Statistics Office, 65
Chrysler, 107
Civil Service, 28–9, 34
  listing, 101
  Pay Research Unit, 70–1
  salary structure in, 58
  and trade unions, 41, 50, 53
Civil Service Union, 87
clerical jobs, 14, 21–2, 78, 83, 86, 124
  and productivity schemes, 94
Cobol proficiency courses, 61
collective bargaining, Ch. 6
  collective agreement, 47
  by computer, Ch. 8
  and data-processing staff, 47–55
  information required for, 69–71
  Procedure Agreement, 46–7, 61
  see also negotiations
collectivity, 7
Common Market, 20, 43–4, 64, 109, 115
Community Policy for Data Processing, 115
computer appreciation courses, 61
computer bureaux, 5, 8, 12–13, 15, 16, 21, 83
  and trade unions, 54, 62, 84–5, 88–90
computer consultants, 13, 23, 83, 97–8
computer industry, 5, 11, 17, 18, 40, 82, 83
  and collective bargaining, 48–52, 67
  and Common Market, 43–4
  and trade unions, 41, 65–8, 108
computer jargon, 9, 94, 101
computer program writing, 13
computers
  applications of, 10–13, 93–6, 118–19, 124

computers–*continued*
and bargaining data, 69–73
and business concentration, 104–5
costs of, 89
effect on jobs by, 5–6, 13–15, 17, Ch. 9; *see also* redundancy
errors of, 1, 32, 33, 97
linked, 11
obsolescence of, 12
programming of, 4, 23
and salaries, 6
social effects of, 82, Ch. 12, 112–14, 119–26
as tools, 1–3, 8, 103
and trade unions, *see* trade unions
types of, 4–5, 10–11, 21, 115
users of, 13, 15–19
Computers and Privacy, 123
Computer Users' Handbook 1975, 12, 15, 52, 55, 59, 61
concentration of business and services, 104–6
conglomerates, 104–5, 106; *see also* multi-national conglomerates
'consensus method', 98
consumer services, 36–7
containerisation, 18, 27
corporate strategy, and computers, 23–4
cost accounting, 25
Courtaulds, 22
credit cards, 5, 17, 83
credit-rating agencies, 35
Critical Path Analysis, 24, 117

data,
standardisation of, 3, 22–3, 107
verification of, 8
data-banks, 29, 34–6, 42, 86, 89, 100, 110
of agreements, 73, 88
of medical records, 97
of salaries, 73–4
data-bases, *see* data-banks
Data Processing Managers Association, 11
data processing staff,
and collective bargaining, 47–8
and computer errors, 32–3
job titles and content of, 51, 56–8, 60
mobility of, 49
recruitment of, 52
salary and grading structure of, 49–50, 54–5, 57–61
and trade unions, 53–4, 61–2
of trade unions, 89
training of, *see* training
see also Electronic Data Processing (EDP) department
Data Protective Committee, 123
dentists, 33
Department of Employment, 61, 71
Department of the Environment, 29, 33
Department of Industry, 65, 68
Department of Trade, 33
developing countries, 110, 122, 126, 127
distribution sector, 15, 17–18
and computer use, 27–8
employment in, 39
Driving Licence Centre, Swansea, 30, 33, 35

early retirement schemes, 80
Electrical, Electronic, Telecommunications and Plumbing Union (EETPU), 47, 71, 87, 89
Electronic Data Processing (EDP) department, 15, 21–2, 26–7
and collective bargaining, 47
electronics, 40
Elliot (GEC), 64, 66
employees, *see* labour force
employment, changes in, 39–45
employment agencies, 50, 52–3
Employment Protection Act, 54, 67, 74, 94
Engineering Employers Federation, 70
ETUC, 109
European Economic Community (EEC), *see* Common Market

Ferranti, 64, 66
fidelity bonding, 100–1
Fire, Auto and Marine Insurance Company, 34
Ford, 16, 22, 53, 108
foreman, 117
Friendly Societies, 31, 85, 88
fringe benefits, 50–1, 52, 59–60

Galbraith, J. K., 36
Gas and Electricity Boards, 65
GEC, 21
General and Municipal Workers Union, 89
gigantism, 113
Giro systems, 6, 17, 83

Government Central Computer
Agency, 18
government sector, 15, 18
and computers, 28–30
employment in, 39
largeness in, 106
Greater London Council, 65

Hoffman La Roche, 107
Honeywell, 64, 66
housing system, 82

ICI, 22, 53
industrial action, 70, 73, 105
Industry Act, 74, 82
inflation, 54–5
information,
centralisation of, 82
checking of, 95–6
disclosure of, 74, 94
dissemination of, 25, 34–5, 76, 115
security and privacy of, 29, 34–5, 73, 97, 114–15, 123
information rationing, 3, 26, 42–3
'in-house' installation, 10, 11–12, 13–15, 16, 32
and computer industry, 48
salary structure for, 49–50
size of, 21
and trade unions, 61, 80
in-job training, 22
Inland Revenue, 29
insurance, 17, 26, 40, 81, 100
International Business Machines (IBM), 12, 22, 44, 64–5, 115
International Computers Ltd (ICL), 44, 64–6, 67, 89
International Labour Organisation (ILO), Convention, 96, 53
international trade secretariats, 109
interviews, 99–100
investment, 38–9
ITT, 107

job advertising, 80
job changes, 78, 83, 110–11, 117–18
job creation, 83
job enrichment, 123
job evaluation, 8, 51–2, 58, 60, 70, 97–9
job titles and descriptions, 51–2, 55, 72, 98

labour force,
checks on, 96–7
and computers, 5–6, 7, 23–4
and management, 7, 13–14
managerial, 42–3
mobility of, 79, 81–3, 117–18, 125
and technology, 6
white-collar, 39–41, 53, 81, 94
Labour Party, 31
Labour Research Department, 73
leasing, 11–12
Leisure Revolution, 129
leisure training schemes, 128
LIFO, 80
line management, 117–18
Litton Industries, 107
local government, 18–19, 29, 53, 58, 106
London Airport, 27
London University, 12
Luddites, 6

Macmillan, Harold, 122
management and labour force, 7, 13–14
management information systems, 3, 25–6
Manpower Services Commission, 18, 29, 82–3, 126
manufacturing sector,
and computers, 15–17, 20–6, 124
employment in, 39
number of employees in, 20, 22
profits and investment in, 38–9
'measured day work', 95
medical examinations, 97
mergers and takeovers, 3, 9, 20, 26, 40, 42, 79, 103
merit payments, 60–1, 96
Meteorological Office, 65
Metropolitan Police, 65
Midland Bank, 58
mini-computer, 21, 82, 89, 90, 115, 123
Ministry of Defence, 29
multinational conglomerates and companies, 3–4, 16, 20, 106–9, 119–20, 127, 128

NALGO, 47, 86
National Coal Board, 41
National Computer Centre, Norwich, 30
National Council for Civil Liberties, 34

National Data Processing Service, 12
National Economic Development Office, 74–5
National Enterprise Board, 66
National Health Service, 18, 29, 117
National Insurance payments, 21, 88
National and Local Government Officers Association, 53
National Research Centre, 76
National Union of Miners, 41
negotiations, 46–7, 69–74, 90, 106
New Earnings Survey, 1975, 59
New South Wales Builders' Labourers' Federation, 35
Norwich Union Insurance Company, 38
numerically controlled machines (NCM), 25, 78, 81
NUPE, 89

oligopoly, 16, 105
'on-line' terminals, 11, 21, 86, 90, 113, 115
operations analysis, 101
Organisation and Methods (O & M), 24

Parkinsonian theory of data processing, 79
petro-chemicals, 39, 40
piecerates, 81, 92–3, 95
Planning Agreement system, 43, 68, 74–6, 82, 101
political systems, 112, 127–8
pollution, 119
postal balloting, 87–8
Post Office, 17, 18, 34, 35, 65
  Giro, 6, 83
print unions and printing industry, 17, 81–2
PRISM, 29
private sector, 16, 48, 53, 71
Procedure Agreement, *see* collective bargaining
production line working, 24, 93, 95
production methods, 24–5
productivity schemes, 8, 24–5, 80, 81, 92–4
Professional and Executive Register, 29, 52
professional unions, 62–3
profits, 126
  and investment, 38–9
promotion, *see* assessment and promotion
Protestant work ethic, 128
Prudential Assurance Company, 11, 53, 58
public investment programmes, 79
public sector, 16, 48, 54, 71

'quality of life', 113, 119

'real-time' computers, 10–11, 17, 26, 33, 72, 115
redundancy, 5–6, 8, 14, 21, 27–8, 65, Ch. 9, 127
  and collective bargaining, 47
  voluntary, 80
Regional Health Authorities, 18, 29
Research and Development, 25, 29, 65–6
resource depletion, 118–19
retailing, 18, 28
Retail Price Index, 54, 55, 71
retraining, 79, 80, 82, 83, 118, 125–6, 128
road haulage, 17, 27
Rolls-Royce, 16, 62
Ruskin College, 73

salary structure, 49–50, 54–5, 57–61
  computerised comparison of, 73–4
  see also data-processing staff
Scottish Office Computer Service, 65
seat bookings, 3, 26, 33
Selective Employment Tax, 39
service sector, 15, 17
  and computers, 26–7, 124
  employment in, 39, 43
Sex Discrimination Act, 99
shift work, 56
shipping, 17, 27–8, 40–1, 81
'shopping basket approach', 74
silicon chips, 82, 89, 115
staff associations, 61
status, 62–3
stock analysis and control, 25, 28, 36
Stock Exchange, 17
stress, 113, 116–17, 122
supermarkets, 18, 28, 36
Swedish Labour Market, 83
sympathy strikes, 48

TASS, 87
taxation, 21, 29, 54, 59, 88
  corporate, 38, 119, 126–7
technological redundancy, *see* redundancy
'temps', 50, 52
TGWU, 47, 71

time-sharing, 13, 15
Trade Union Congress (TUC), 63, 73, 84, 109
trade unions,
administration of, 88, 90
administrative units of, 85–7
balloting, *see* postal balloting
checks on computer decisions by, 101–2
and collective bargaining, 46–8, 69–71
communications in, 87–8
and computer industry, 65–8
and computers, 6–9, 13, 29, 30, 35–6, 39–42 *passim*, 69–76
computer use by, Ch. 10
and conglomerates and mergers, 106, 108–9, 115–16
and data-processing staff, 53–4, 59, 60
and employment agencies, 52–3
function and objectives of, 6–7, 31, 35, 63
and job evaluation, 98–9
and Labour Party, 31
members of, 31–2
and productivity schemes, 94–5
recognition of, 61, 67
recruitment by, 41–3, 61–3
Research Department of, 69, 71, 94–5
subscription rates and collection system of, 85–6
and technological redundancy, 79–83
and transitional systems, 127–8
and white-collar sector, 62–3
training, 57–8, 61, 76, 83, 110, 118, 125
transfer-pricing, 107

unemployment, 39, 65, 124–5, 126–7, 129
Unidata, 44
Unilever, 12, 22
Union of Post Office Workers (UPW), 35
Univac, 64, 66
university computers, 12, 18, 29, 53
University Computer Staffs dispute, 53
USDAW, 89

Vehicle Licensing Centre, Swansea, 18
vertical integration, 105–6

wealth, concentration and distribution of, 113–14, 119, 128
Westin, Robert, 34
white-collar sector, *see* labour force, white-collar
wholesaling, 28
workers' participation, 115, 119
work-sharing, 79, 125, 126, 128

Younger Committee, 34, 114